Nightcap

A Play

Francis Durbridge

Samuel French – London
New York – Sydney – Toronto – Hollywood

NIGHTCAP

First produced at the Yvonne Arnaud Theatre, Guildford on 6th July 1983. The play was presented in association with Triumph-Apollo Productions Ltd, with the following cast of characters:

Sarah Radford	Nyree Dawn Porter
Geoffrey Curtis	Robin Halstead
Lucy Baker	Christine Russell
Edward Donnington	Maitland Chandler
Kate Warren	Barbara Murray
Jack Radford	Jack Hedley
Anna Truman	Suzanne Church
Dr Maurice Young	John Clegg
Cliff Jordan	Derek Waring
Arnold Boston	Jeremy Hawk

The play directed by Val May

The action of the play takes place in Sarah and Jack Radford's house in East Sussex

ACT I SCENE 1 Late afternoon—early November
       SCENE 2 Three months later—a Tuesday night
       SCENE 3 Wednesday morning
       SCENE 4 Thursday night
       SCENE 5 Friday morning

ACT II SCENE 1 Friday morning
       SCENE 2 Friday evening
       SCENE 3 Saturday morning
       SCENE 4 Six months later—morning

Time—the present

For Simon

ACT I*

SCENE I

The living-room and sun-lounge of a large house in East Sussex. The house stands in just over four acres. It is late afternoon

Since Sarah Radford inherited the house from her father the sun-lounge has been added and the living-room modernized. The sun-lounge is at an angle to the main room and has a large window with full-length curtains, and a patio door leading into the garden. The furnishings in the living-room are mostly antique, but there are modern pieces, including a desk, a table with telephone, ashtray, cigarette box, etc., also coffee tables with lamps, and a drinks cabinet over which there is a large portrait of Sarah's husband, Jack Radford

There is a door DL leading to a study but the main entrance to the living-room is through the wall R. The rest of this wall is adorned with works of art and leather-bound volumes of unread classics. Part of the hall, and a section of the staircase leading to the rest of the house, can be seen through the open doorway

When the CURTAIN rises, Sarah Radford is standing by the desk, searching through one of the drawers. She fails to find what she is looking for and, obviously worried, noisily closes the drawer and opens yet another one

She is looking through this drawer when . . . Geoffrey Curtis enters. Geoffrey is in his early thirties; he wears glasses and has a nervous habit of constantly adjusting them, sometimes taking them off and staring at the lenses. He carries a briefcase

Sarah (*surprised*) Why, hallo, Geoffrey!

Geoffrey Sorry if I'm disturbing you, Mrs Radford.

Sarah What can I do for you?

Geoffrey I was hoping to have a word with Jack, but I gather he's not home yet.

Sarah No, I'm afraid he isn't. But I'm expecting him. What time did he leave the office?

Geoffrey (*adjusting his glasses as he moves down to Sarah*) He went to a Council meeting at ten o'clock this morning—since when we haven't seen him.

Sarah Oh . . .

Geoffrey Perhaps you'd ask him to give me a ring. I shall be in all evening.

Sarah Yes, of course.

---

*N.B. Paragraph 3 on page ii of this Acting Edition regarding photocopying and video-recording should be carefully read.

Geoffrey It's not urgent, but—we've had a spot of bother at the office.

Sarah Again?

Geoffrey Yes, again.

Sarah I'll tell him. Apart from that, how are things at Donnington's these days?

Geoffrey Pretty brisk. We sold several houses at the weekend.

Sarah And how are you, Geoffrey? Have you had a check-up recently?

Geoffrey I saw the doctor about a fortnight ago. He seemed pleased with me, but he still won't let me smoke.

Sarah (*still searching for the missing document*) Quite right too, after all the trouble you've had. Now, if you'll excuse me. Things are a little hectic around here at the moment. It's our Drama Club dinner tonight and I'm making a speech. At least, I hope I'm making a speech! I've lost the wretched thing. (*She turns back to the drawer*) Heaven only knows what I did with it!

Lucy Baker, the Radford's housekeeper, enters from the patio. She has several sheets of notepaper in her hand

Lucy I've found what you're looking for, Mrs Radford.

Sarah (*with relief*) Oh—thank goodness for that! Where did I put it?

Lucy It was in the studio. On top of the piano.

Sarah When did I go into the studio?

Lucy Just after lunch. I saw you. I was in the garden. Don't you remember?

Sarah Yes, of course! How stupid of me. . . .

Geoffrey (*faintly amused*) I'll say good-bye.

Sarah (*turning, suddenly aware of him again*) Oh—good-bye, Geoffrey. I'll get Jack to phone you.

Geoffrey exits

Sarah moves to Lucy and takes the notepaper from her

I was just beginning to panic. I really thought I'd lost it. (*She looks at the notepaper*) Oh dear!

Lucy Now what's the matter?

Sarah It's a very dull speech, I'm afraid.

Lucy You say that every year!

Sarah Katie Warren ought to be making the speech, not me! She's the President of the Society. I'm just the Secretary. But she always seems to wriggle out of these things. I don't know how she manages it.

The telephone rings

You answer it, Lucy.

Lucy crosses to the desk while Sarah studies her speech

Lucy (*on the phone*) Hallo? . . . Yes, it is. . . . Who is it speaking? . . . I'm sorry, I can't hear you. . . . (*Pause. She looks at Sarah*) It's long distance. . . . I think it's the man I spoke to this morning . . .

Sarah Oh! I'd better talk to him. (*She crosses to Lucy, puts her speech down, and takes the phone*)

Lucy goes into the sun-lounge. During Sarah's phone conversation she tidies the room and eventually, prior to drawing the curtains, stands looking out into the garden

(*On the phone*) Hallo? . . . This is Mrs Radford speaking. . . . I'm sorry my husband isn't here. . . . Yes, I know, you spoke to my housekeeper. . . . Didn't you try the office, she gave you the number? . . . Oh. Oh, I see. . . . Yes I'm expecting him at any moment. . . . What did you say your name was? . . . Montserrat? . . . Yes, of course I'll deliver a message, Mr Montserrat. What is it you want me to tell my husband? (*Slight pause*) I beg your pardon? I'm sorry, I didn't quite . . . (*she is taken aback*) Three more people have—*what*? . . . Died? . . . (*She stares at the phone in astonishment*)

Lucy (*suddenly, at the window*) I think this is Mr Radford . . .

Lucy crosses into the living-room and exits into the hall

Sarah (*on the phone, quickly, looking towards the hall*) My husband has just arrived. If you hold on I'll get him to speak to you. . . . (*she puts the receiver down and turns away from the table*)

Pause

Lucy enters

Lucy It's not Mr Radford. It's your brother.
Sarah Edward! It can't be!
Lucy It is! It's Mr Donnington. He's just getting rid of the taxi. He seems to have a lot of things with him. Shall I put them in the studio?
Sarah What? Yes, yes, do that. . . . No, wait! Put them in the guest room, he can sort them out later. (*She is flustered*) I thought Edward was in New York, I had a card from him only. . . . Why on earth didn't he let me know he was coming!
Lucy Not to worry. We'll manage . . .

Lucy exits

Sarah returns to the table and picks up the phone

Sarah (*her thoughts elsewhere*) I'm sorry, I was mistaken, it wasn't my husband. . . . Yes, I will. . . . Yes, of course. . . . (*She replaces the phone and moves towards the hall*)

Pause

Edward Donnington enters. He is a well-known concert pianist; a tired-looking man. He joins Sarah and embraces her

Edward Sarah!
Sarah This is a lovely surprise, Edward! But I thought you were still in New York?
Edward I left New York on Sunday. I've been in Spain most of this week.
Sarah On holiday?
Edward (*hesitantly*) No, not exactly.

Sarah (*looking at Edward anxiously*) You look to me as if you could do with a holiday.

Edward I'm tired, that's all. We were held up in Madrid and then when we arrived at Heathrow. . . . Well, you know what Heathrow's like.

Tiny pause

Sarah (*still looking at him*) I got your card. What really happened in New York?

Edward (*tired of the question*) What happened? I told you. They didn't like me.

Sarah But you've always been so successful in America!

Edward (*irritated*) Not this time, Sarah. I was a flop. I played badly and the critics, quite rightly, went for me. It's as simple as that.

Sarah I wish you'd told me you were coming, Edward. I've got to spend this evening in London. It's our Drama Club dinner and I'm making a speech. I can't very well get out of it.

Edward (*with an affectionate gesture*) Don't be silly! Of course you can't get out of it.

Sarah I'll be very late back, I'm afraid.

Edward Not to worry. It looks as if I'm going to be around for some time. You'll see quite enough of me, Sarah. Jack's going with you, I take it?

Sarah No, Jack wouldn't be found dead at this sort of thing. In any case, I won't have him near me when I'm making a speech. He makes me nervous. Kate Warren's picking me up.

Edward Katie! How is she?

Sarah She's fine.

Edward Does she still give those terrible dinner parties?

Sarah Yes, and what's worse she's now giving cookery lessons

Edward Cookery lessons?

Sarah On the box. "Out of the Frying Pan" with Katie Warren. She's quite famous these days.

Edward I was on the loo for three hours after one of her dinner parties— and I still came out in a rash. The doctor said he'd never seen anything like it. My body looked like a map of Outer Mongolia.

Sarah (*laughing*) I remember. You should hear Jack on Katie's cooking!

Pause

Edward is hesitating, undecided whether to mention what is obviously on his mind. Finally, he makes a decision

Edward I spoke to Jack a couple of days ago. Did he tell you?

Sarah (*surprised*) No.

Edward He—didn't mention it?

Sarah No, he didn't.

Edward I telephoned him from Madrid. I was concerned. Very concerned. I still am.

Sarah (*puzzled*) About what?

Edward About the business. Donnington's.

Sarah You must want something to worry about if you're worried about

Donnington's! They sold more properties last year than ever before. Why Jack even sold The Grange to those terrible people, the Hoskins.

Edward Yes, well—I think we know how that deal was done!

Sarah (*annoyed*) Do we, Edward? (*A moment, then:*) If you must know I talked to Jack about Carol Hoskins. I had it out with him. And for your information, he is *not* having an affair with her!

Edward (*slightly regretting his remark*) I'm glad to hear it . . .

Sarah Our Carol's the one with the money. She's loaded. Jack discovered this very early on in the negotiations and played up to her like mad. That's all there was to it.

Edward That's as maybe. But I still don't think you realize what's happening. Jack's taking risks, unnecessary risks, and I don't like it.

Sarah What sort of risks? What are you referring to?

Edward (*hesitating*) I'll talk to Jack about it.

Sarah Talk to me. If you're worried about the firm I've a right to know what's worrying you.

Edward No—I'm sorry I mentioned it. We'll discuss it later.

A slightly strained silence

Sarah When father died and we inherited Donnington's we agreed—we both agreed—that although you and I owned the business Jack should have a completely free hand in the running of it.

Edward I'm aware of that, Sarah. (*He moves away from her*)

Sarah Jack made it quite clear, right from the start, that if there was any interference from us . . .

Edward (*quickly; turning*) Sarah, I don't want to interfere! What the devil do I know about running an estate agents? I'm not a business man, I'm a musician. Although there seems to be some doubt about even that these days. It's just that . . . (*A moment; then turning away from her again*) Let's talk about it tomorrow.

Sarah (*quietly; concerned*) Yes, let's do that.

Kate Warren enters from the hall

Kate Why Edward! My dear . . . (*She crosses to Edward and kisses him*)

Edward Hallo, Kate.

Kate How nice to see you again, after all this time! (*She stares at the dress Sarah is wearing*)

Sarah (*puzzled*) What is it, Kate?

Edward looks at Kate

Kate Nothing. Nothing, darling. Why on earth didn't you tell me you were expecting Edward?

Sarah I wasn't expecting him—and he's only just this minute arrived!

Edward You look well, Kate.

Kate I am well.

Edward You never seem to change. You look exactly the same as you did five years ago.

Kate Make it ten, darling, and I'll fall for it! You must come and have a meal one evening, Edward. I'll arrange a little party for you.

Edward Er–thank you Kate. That's very kind of you, but I've got a pretty hectic time ahead of me and . . .

Kate You won't be asked to play, I promise you! . . .

Edward (*with a little laugh*) Well—in that case, I'll look forward to it. (*To Sarah*) Don't worry about tonight, Sarah. You'll be a huge success. You always are.

Kate Of course she'll be a success! She's marvellous. She really is. She had them rolling in the aisles last year. I'll let you know about the dinner party, Edward.

Edward Yes—do that, Katie.

Edward exits

Sarah (*quickly*) What is it, Kate? Why did you stare at me like that?

Kate moves nearer to Sarah, pointing at her dress

Kate That dress! Where did you get it from? Don't tell me! Hildegarde?

Sarah Yes.

Kate She sold me the same dress yesterday afternoon. (*She stares at the dress*) Exactly the same! Identical!

Sarah (*laughing*) Well, thank goodness you're not wearing it!

Kate The little bitch! I'll bet she did it deliberately . . .

Sarah Of course she didn't

Kate Of course she did! You don't know Hildegarde like I do! She has a horrendous sense of humour. A friend of mine told me she laughed like a drain when that casserole of mine caught fire on the box. (*She takes a good look at Sarah*) Anyway, I'll say one thing. You look a great deal better in it than I do. (*A moment; then with a nod towards the hall*) Edward doesn't seem very happy.

Sarah Is it surprising?

Kate No, I suppose not. Did you see the American notices?

Sarah shakes her head

They were very nasty, I'm afraid. Quite cruel some of them.

Sarah Yes, well—don't worry. Edward will bounce back. He always does.

Kate I think we ought to be making a move, Sarah. The traffic's pretty heavy this time of day.

Sarah I'm ready. I told Lucy we'd give her a lift as far as the station.

Kate Yes, of course. How is the Lucy situation? Is the battle over?

Sarah For the time being.

Kate What happened?

Sarah Need you ask? We lost as usual. I used to say "I don't know what I'd do without her." Now—she has so much time off, I'm beginning to find out.

Jack Radford enters. He takes off his coat and tosses it onto a chair

Jack Sorry I'm late, Sarah, my love. (*He kisses her*) Hallo, Kate! Burnt any casseroles lately? (*To Sarah*) I've been sitting in that wretched Council

Chamber since ten o'clock this morning. (*He crosses to the drinks cabinet*) Lucy tells me Edward's arrived.

Sarah Yes.

Jack Were you expecting him?

Sarah No, of course not. I'd have told you. I was amazed when he turned up.

Jack How long is he staying? (*He looks at the bottles, undecided whether to have a drink or not*)

Sarah You know Edward. It could be a week, it could be twenty-four hours. By the way, you've just missed Geoffrey.

Jack Thank God, for that! I see quite enough of that young man during office hours. What did he want?

Sarah There's been some trouble at the office.

Jack When isn't there trouble at the office?

Sarah (*picking up her speech*) He wants you to ring him.

Jack Yes, well—he's unlucky. That hypochondriac doesn't seem to be able to take care of a damn thing these days. Except himself. I'll talk to him tomorrow. (*He picks up the decanter of sherry*)

Sarah Oh—and there was a message for you, Jack. A rather curious one, from someone called Montserrat.

Jack Montserrat? (*He puts the decanter down*)

Sarah He phoned twice. We gave him the office number but they said you were out.

Jack Montserrat? (*Moving down to Sarah*) I don't know anyone by that name.

Sarah It was a long-distance call.

Jack What was the message?

Sarah He said, "Tell your husband, three more people have died . . ."

Jack (*still moving down to her; bewildered*) Three more people have died?

Sarah Yes.

A moment. Jack is still staring at Sarah

Jack I don't get this. What did he mean?

Sarah I don't know.

Jack Was it a joke of some kind?

Sarah I—I don't think so.

Jack It must have been.

Sarah It didn't sound like a joke. Not the way the man said it.

Jack I've never heard of anyone called Montserrat. (*Puzzled*) It was a long-distance call, you say?

Sarah Yes.

Jack From where?

Sarah I don't know.

Jack I just can't imagine what he was talking about.

Kate He was probably a nutter; a screwball. The world's full of them.

Jack That's about it, if you ask me.

Kate You should hear some of the calls I get, especially after one of my cookery lessons.

Lucy appears, wearing outdoor clothes

Lucy I'm ready when you are, Mrs Radford.
Sarah Wait for us in the car, Lucy.

Lucy picks up Jack's coat and exits

Sarah moves to Jack and kisses him

Be nice to Edward, try not to fall out with him.
Jack Why should I fall out with him?
Sarah (*after a tiny pause*) He's very much on edge; he's had a bad time lately.
Jack I know. Dont't worry. We'll have a few drinks and then pop along to the *Brasserie*.
Kate Ye gods! Poor Edward ...
Jack You're a snob, Katie. I like the *Brasserie*, and so does Edward.
Kate (*shaking her head*) French food to throw away!
Sarah (*laughing*) Come along!

Sarah exits with Kate

Jack returns to the drinks cabinet and, somewhat annoyed, pours himself a drink. He finishes the drink then, after a momentary hesitation, makes a decision and crosses to the phone. As he reaches the table Edward can be heard "trying out" the piano in the studio. Jack stands for a moment, listening—then he picks up the phone and dials a long-distance number. Pause. The piano stops. Jack's eyes are now on the hall in case Edward appears

Jack (*suddenly; on the phone*) Hallo? ... Hallo? ... I'm sorry I can't hear you! ... That's better! ... This is Jack Radford, I want to speak to Señor Montserrat. It's urgent, put me through straight away! (*Pause*). ... Is that you, Charles? ... Jack. ... What the hell are you playing at, leaving a message with my wife! ... What? ... No, no, of course she doesn't! ... Well, don't do it again, for God's sake! ... Now tell me about the three deaths. ... Who were they? ... (*Pause*) Two Spaniards and a Belgian? ... Well, that's a relief. ... (*Slight pause*) What's that? ... Yes, yes, of course, we're going ahead with the Malaga project, but you know what banks are like, they're always hellishly long winded. ... Yes, I'm sure they will, but these things take time. ... No, no, don't ring me, I'll phone you at the end of the week. ... (*He puts down the phone, returns to the drinks cabinet and mixes himself a drink*)

Edward enters from the patio

The two men take each other in

Jack Hallo, Edward. I didn't expect to see you so soon after that somewhat acrimonious phone call.
Edward I should have let Sarah know I was coming. If you've no objection, I'd like to use the studio for a little while—a week perhaps.
Jack The studio is yours, to use whenever you feel like it, you know that.
Edward Thank you. (*A moment, then:*) May I help myself to a drink?

Jack Let me get it for you. What would you like? Scotch?
Edward Thank you.

Jack fixes the drink and takes it down to Edward

Slight pause

Jack What were you doing in Madrid? Giving a recital?
Edward I went to see an old friend of mine. He's head of the Spanish Bank Corporation.
Jack You always seem to know the right people, don't you, Edward?
Edward It's sometimes necessary. If I were you I'd cultivate the habit.
Jack What's that supposed to mean?
Edward It means you'd be well advised to disassociate yourself—and Donnington's—from operators like Charles Montserrat.
Jack Is that why you saw your friend in Madrid, to check up on Montserrat?
Edward That was one reason. I also wanted to know to what extent—if any—Donnington's were involved in the Valencia disaster.
Jack Why didn't you ask me that question, instead of going behind my back?
Edward I did. You lied. You said you'd never heard of Charles Montserrat and that Donnington's had nothing whatsoever to do with the property.
Jack (*shaking his head*) No, no, I said nothing of the sort. It was a very bad line, you obviously misunderstood me. Now look, Edward, I don't want to fall out with you, that's the last thing I want to do. But your phone call annoyed me. Annoyed me intensely—so much so in fact that I didn't even mention it to Sarah. (*He makes a quick decision*) Now let me put you in the picture so there's no longer any misunderstanding between us. To be honest, to be perfectly honest, yes—I do know Montserrat. And I agree, he's an operator. Of course he's an operator! All those boys are. But so far as this Valencia business is concerned. . . . (*A shade too affably*) Look, I'll tell you exactly what happened.
Edward I know what happened! The building collapsed. Thirty-two people were killed. And God only knows how many poor devils are still in hospital.
Jack I know. It was dreadful. Appalling. But Donnington's were not responsible for what happened. Not in any way.
Edward How can you say that when, to my knowledge, you sold at least twelve of the apartments?
Jack That's true. But we didn't have a say in the construction of the building. We were merely responsible for . . .
Edward According to my information you did! You met Montserrat and his team in Valencia just over three years ago. You saw the plans, you discussed the specifications, and you surveyed the site.
Jack That's not true! It's just not true!
Edward (*a moment, then:*) Very well. Let's talk about something else. To what extent are you—by which I mean Donnington's—involved in this new operation of Montserrat's? This time-sharing project?

Jack We're not involved. Not in any way. But who told you about this time-sharing project? Was it your banking friend?

Edward Yes.

Jack What else did he tell you?

Edward He said that a British company had expressed an interest in the scheme and had promised to find part of the finance.

Jack Well—it isn't Donnington's. But I'll be frank. I have heard of this project and Montserrat did try and interest us in it. As a matter of fact, he made us a damn good offer.

Edward Which you rejected?

Jack Yes—which we rejected.

A pause. Edward is obviously unconvinced

Don't you believe me?

Edward I'd like to believe you . . .

Jack Then why don't you . . .

Edward . . . I'd also like to see the correspondence.

Jack (*sharply*) The correspondence?

Edward You presumably wrote to Montserrat about the project. I'd like to see copies of the correspondence.

For a moment Jack is taken aback, then anger takes over

Jack What the hell's come over you? You've never doubted my word before! Now let's get one thing straight! *I am* the managing director of Donnington's, even though you and Sarah own the company . . .

Edward Leave Sarah out of this! I simply want to know what you said to Montserrat when you rejected his offer—*if* you did reject it. If you haven't got copies of the letters here we'll go down to the office.

Jack stares at him, even angrier than before, then turning goes quickly into the study

Pause

Edward finishes his drink, then crosses to the drinks cabinet, and pours himself another. He stands by the cabinet, deep in thought

Pause

Jack appears carrying a folder containing many letters. The folder is open and he is reading the correspondence as he enters the room. He stops for a moment, staring at the letters then he looks up and angrily indicates the sofa

Edward crosses to the sofa and is joined by Jack who hands him the folder

Jack Perhaps when you've read this file you'll have the decency to apologize. Only four of the letters refer to the time-sharing project, but in view of your attitude I think you'd better read the lot!

Edward sits and opens the folder Jack watches him, then moves behind the sofa. There is a long pause. Edward is studying the correspondence, hardly aware of Jack's presence. He is obviously somewhat puzzled by the letters.

Jack produces a gun, stares at it for a moment, hesitating—then he points it at Edward's head and takes careful aim. There is a loud explosion. Edward slumps forward on the sofa

Black-out

SCENE 2

The same. Three months later. Ten o'clock at night. A storm has taken place and there is still the sound of rain

Sarah is smoking a cigarette as she restlessly paces the living-room. Her manner is tense and from time to time an almost frightened look appears on her face. Eventually she stops pacing, extinguishes her cigarette, and draws her dressing-gown closer to her body

The front door bell rings

Sarah looks up, hesitates—then rushes out into the hall

Pause

The front door is heard opening and closing, followed by voices

Sarah (*off*) Kate, my dear! Thank you for coming! It's very good of you.
Kate (*off*) What is it, Sarah? What's happened?

Kate enters. She is wearing a headscarf. Sarah follows her into the room

I came as quickly as I could. I was in the bath when you phoned.
Sarah Oh, Kate, I'm sorry! Do forgive me, dragging you out on a night like this!
Kate What is it, Sarah? Are you ill?
Sarah I've got a terrible headache, I've had it all evening, but that's not why I sent for you . . .
Kate Then what's happened? Where's Jack—and Lucy?
Sarah Lucy's in London. She's due back tomorrow morning. Jack's at the Hoskins'.
Kate The Hoskins'! What on earth is Jack doing there?
Sarah He sold Hoskins The Grange and it's their house-warming party. He had to go, he just couldn't get out of it.
Kate Knowing Hoskins it was probably in the contract. Now what's this all about?
Sarah I know you're not going to believe me! (*She paces up and down*) I know you'll think I'm crazy! Perhaps I am—perhaps that's the only possible explanation . . .
Kate (*with a gentle note of authority in her voice*) What is it, Sarah?
Sarah (*tensely*) I—I heard Edward again. It was the same as last time.
Kate What do you mean—you heard Edward? You heard the piano?

Sarah finally stops pacing

Sarah Yes. He was in the studio. I heard him playing, Kate.

Kate (*staring at Sarah*) Edward's dead. You know he is, Sarah.

Sarah (*desperately; shaking her head*) Then who is it I keep hearing? Who is it?

Kate (*softly*) I don't know.

Sarah Am I going out of my mind? Is that the explanation? Is that what's happening?

Kate Of course you're not going out of your mind. Don't be absurd! But it's the third time this has happened. I think perhaps you should consult someone. . . .

Sarah I've seen Dr Young.

Kate Yes, well—you know my opinion of Maurice. (*She studies Sarah; then curiously*) What happened tonight? Where were you when you thought you heard the piano?

Sarah I did hear it! I swear I did!

Kate Where were you?

Sarah I was upstairs in the bedroom. It *was* Edward. I know it was Edward! He was playing Schumann, the piece he played at the Festival Hall the night . . .

Kate What happened exactly?

Sarah As soon as I heard the piano I raced downstairs and went straight to the studio. There was no one there. The room was empty.

Kate Could you still hear the piano?

Sarah No. It stopped just as I reached the hall.

Kate Is that what happened on the previous occasions?

Sarah It's what happened last time, except that I was in the dining-room and it was four o'clock in the afternoon. Jack was at the office. Lucy was out shopping. (*After a moment's consideration*) But the first time, the first time was different . . .

Kate In what way, different?

Sarah It was a Sunday, about a month after the inquest . . . Jack was sitting on the sofa reading the papers. I was in the kitchen. Suddenly I heard the piano. I knew it was Edward! I knew immediately. I cried out, dropped what I was doing, and rushed in here. Jack stared at me as if I'd taken leave of my senses . . .

Kate He'd heard nothing?

Sarah Nothing! the poor man was bewildered.

Pause

Kate You say you've told Maurice about this?

Sarah Yes, but he wasn't very helpful. He simply gave me some awful medicine and told me to forget all about it. Later, when he and Jack were talking I overheard him say something about me being very highly strung, like Edward . . .

Kate What nonsense! Your brother was a lovely person and I was terribly fond of him, you know that. Now for heaven's sake, don't start getting silly ideas about yourself. You're one of the most level-headed women I've ever met.

Sarah Thank you, Kate. That's what I wanted to hear.

Kate Now if you take my advice, you'll try and forget what happened to Edward. The fact that he took his own life is unimportant. Just remember how talented he was and the enormous amount of pleasure he gave to everyone.

Sarah Yes, that's what I keep telling myself, but . . . (*with anguish*) Why did he do it, Kate? Why did he do such a terrible thing?

Kate You know why! We must have talked about this a hundred times during the past three months! You were at the inquest. You confirmed Jack's evidence about Edward being depressed and worried about the future. It was you that told the Coroner about the traumatic experience your brother had in New York . . .

Sarah (*miserably*) Yes, I know, I know. I'm sorry, Katie. (*A moment, then:*) Jack's worried about me. I know he is. He wants me to see an old school friend of his, a psychiatrist. They play squash together. (*She sits on the arm of the sofa*)

Kate (*moving down to Sarah*) I think that's a splendid idea.

Sarah (*shaking her head*) I hate the thought of getting involved with a shrink.

Kate My dear, a shrink who plays squash can't possibly do anybody any harm. Besides, you mustn't believe everything you read about psychiatrists. I went to one once and he . . .

Sarah You did?

Kate Yes, and he did me a power of good. Although I question whether he ever played squash. Not that he needed to. (*Silencing her with a little laugh*) It was a long time ago, and that's all—positively all—I'm going to tell you about it. (*A slight hesitation, then:*) Sarah, forgive my asking, I know it's none of my business, but—did Edward's death affect Donnington's in any way?

Sarah Donnington's? Why, no. I inherited his shares, of course, which means I now own the company . . . (*She stops; with curiosity*) But why are you interested in Donnington's?

Kate I went to see Arnold Boston the other day. You know Arnold . . .

Sarah Yes, of course . . .

Kate He's my lawyer and I consult him from time to time. After we'd had our meeting he asked how you were and, inevitably I'm afraid, we talked about Edward. Then, just as I was leaving, he made—what I thought— was a very odd remark.

Sarah Oh?

Kate He said: "What's happening to Donnington's, Kate? What's the rapacious Mr Radford up to, now that Edward's no longer with us?"

Sarah What on earth did he mean?

Kate I don't know.

Sarah (*a moment; puzzled*) Rapacious? What a curious word to use . . .

Tiny pause

Kate I gather you never see Arnold these days?

Sarah No. We used to see a great deal of each other at one time. Then he

and Jack had a row. Don't ask me what it was about. I never did find out.
It was sad really.

Kate He's had a bad time just recently, I'm afraid. His wife's been terribly
ill. She still is.

Sarah Oh, I am sorry. Arnold thinks the world of her. He must be very
worried.

Kate He is, poor darling. Look, Sarah, if I were you I wouldn't wait up for
Jack. Take a couple of aspirins and go to bed.

Sarah Yes, I think perhaps I will. And thank you for coming, Katie.

The front door opens and closes

I felt I just had to talk to someone. (*She quickly turns towards the hall*)

Jack enters. He looks agitated as he quickly disposes of his raincoat

Jack (*surprised*) Hallo, Kate! What are you doing here?

Kate (*to Sarah*) Now that's what I call a really friendly greeting! Not "drop
dead"—or "get lost"—just a nice, warm, "What are you doing here?"

Sarah rises

Jack I'm sorry, Kate. I didn't mean to be rude.

Sarah What is it, Jack? Is anything wrong?

Jack I'm just exasperated, that's all. You know the effect Hoskins has on
me! (*To Kate*) You can't get a word in edgeways. He corners you the
moment you arrive, and that's it for the rest of the evening.

Kate The house-warming was not a success, I gather?

Jack Not with me, it wasn't! But I must say he's a generous old bore. I've
never seen so much booze.

Kate Paid for by Mrs Hoskins, no doubt?

Jack I wouldn't know about that.

Kate What was our Carol wearing on this auspicious occasion? Mink
leotards?

Jack I really didn't notice. (*He moves down to the sofa, then stops—looking
first at Kate, then at his wife*) Are you all right, Sarah? Did you send for
Katie?

Sarah No, I . . .

Kate I phoned Sarah, just to have a chat. She said she was on her own so I
said I'd pop round.

Jack Oh. Oh, I see. (*He looks at her headscarf*)

Kate (*after a faintly awkward pause, conscious of the fact that Jack is looking
at her headscarf*) Is it still raining?

Jack No, it's stopped.

Kate Thank goodness for that. 'Bye, Sarah. I'll give you a ring later in the
week. Take good care of her, Jack.

Kate smiles at both of them and exits

Sarah Kate's been telling me about Irene Boston. I hadn't the slightest idea
she was so ill.

Jack completely ignores what Sarah is saying, quickly crosses towards her and takes hold of her arm

Jack Sarah, my love, listen. I don't want to worry you—that's the last thing I want to do! But something happened tonight, something awful. . .
Sarah (*alarmed*) What is it Jack?
Jack I knocked someone down. A girl . . . she ran across the road, right in front of me. . . . The car skidded and . . .
Sarah Is she badly hurt?
Jack I—I don't know. I don't think so, but I'm not sure.

As Jack releases her arm Sarah looks at him, puzzled

Sarah You're not sure?
Jack I—I daren't send for the police, I daren't report it to anyone . . .
Sarah Why ever not?
Jack I've been drinking, all evening, since seven o'clock. I'd never pass a test, I'd be way over the top. Besides, you know what people would say, what the local rag would make of it. They're always ready to dig up that other business.
Sarah But what happened to the girl? You didn't just leave her?
Jack No—No—I. . . . There was no one about, no one saw the accident, so I telephoned Maurice, from a call box. I told him I wanted to see him. He said he had a call to make but he'd get here as soon as he could.
Sarah But what's happened to the girl?
Jack She's outside, in my car. I brought her here. I just didn't know what the devil to do.
Sarah (*softly; with a note of compassion*) Oh, Jack . . .

Jack stares at her for a moment, then turns and goes quickly out into the hall

Sarah is worried and a shade bewildered. She makes as if to follow Jack, then changes her mind. After a moment she goes into the sun-lounge and collects a rug and several cushions. She brings them down to the sofa and arranges the cushions

Jack returns. He is carrying Anna Truman, a good-looking girl in her late twenties

Jack It seems to be her shoulder. I hope it's not serious.
Sarah I'll get some brandy . . .

As Jack carries the girl to the sofa, Sarah crosses to the drinks cabinet and pours a glass of brandy

Jack (*lowering Anna onto the sofa*) I don't think we'd better give her anything to drink, not before Maurice gets here.
Sarah Surely, brandy won't do her any harm . . .
Jack I think we'd better wait.

Sarah hesitates, then puts the glass down and rejoins Jack at the sofa. There is a slight pause

Sarah Who is she, do you know?
Jack I've no idea.

Anna stirs, making a sound

Sarah What's she saying?
Jack (*to Anna*) What is it, my dear?

Pause. Anna murmurs again. Jack looks at Sarah and shakes his head

Sarah We'll have to find out who she is, Jack.
Jack Her handbag's in the car, that may help us. I'll take a look at it later.

Sarah moves nearer the sofa and stares at the girl whose eyes are closed

Sarah There's a name on the chain she's wearing . . .
Jack (*peering at the chain*) Anna . . .
Anna (*moving and finally opening her eyes*) Where am I? What's—what's happened?
Jack You've been involved in an accident. You're not badly hurt but— we've sent for a doctor.
Anna An accident? (*Alarmed*) Who are you? What am I doing here? (*She attempts to move; she winces with pain*)
Sarah Is it your shoulder?
Anna Yes. I—I have difficulty moving it. (*She makes another attempt to move, crying out in pain*)
Jack Try not to move. A doctor will be here soon I promise you.
Anna (*staring at Jack*) I've seen you before somewhere.
Jack My name is Radford. I'm an estate agent. This is my wife. I was on my way home when . . . you ran in front of my car. I did my best to avoid hitting you but the car skidded and . . . I'm terribly sorry, but there was just nothing I could do.

Pause

Anna Yes . . . I remember now. I was sheltering under a tree . . . the storm got worse . . . I was frightened and I dashed across the road . . . (*In pain*) Why didn't you call an ambulance instead of bringing me here?
Jack I—I couldn't find a call box . . .
Anna I see. But why didn't you. . . . (*She attempts to rise, is partly successful, but finally collapses back onto the sofa*)
Jack Please don't try and move. Wait until the doctor arrives. He'll give you something to ease the pain.
Sarah (*after a tiny pause*) Do you live near here?
Anna I—I live in Hove. I'd been visiting friends of mine and my car was parked. . . . (*In pain with her shoulder*) Could you please . . . move one of these cushions . . . ?
Sarah Yes, of course. (*She picks up one of the cushions and places it behind Anna's head*) Is that better?
Anna (*closing her eyes*) Yes, it is. Thank you.

Sarah looks at Anna

Sarah (*softly*) Don't worry, Jack. She'll be all right, I'm sure.

Jack moves away from the sofa. Sarah joins him

(*Quietly*) What did you say to Maurice when you phoned him?
Jack I said I wanted to see him.
Sarah Didn't you tell him about the accident?
Jack No. I simply said it was urgent. Why?

Sarah shakes her head

Why, Sarah?
Sarah He probably thinks you telephoned because of me ...
Jack That's possible, I suppose. I hadn't thought of that. (*He looks at her*) Why was Katie here? Did you send for her?
Sarah No—no, of course not. She told you why she came.
Jack She didn't sound very convincing. (*Still looking at her*) You look tired, Sarah my love, and not at all well.
Sarah I've got a headache, that's all.
Jack Have you taken anything for it?
Sarah No ...
Jack What about taking a dose of that medicine Maurice gave you?
Sarah I threw it away! I'm sick to death of Maurice and his medicine, to say nothing of ... (*She stops*)
Jack What is it?
Sarah He'll ask me about the medicine, he's bound to—you know what he's like! (*She shakes her head*) The very last person I wanted to see tonight was Maurice!
Jack Then why don't you go and lie down for a little while?

Sarah looks across at Anna, hesitating

If I need you, I'll send for you. It'll probably be easier for me anyway, if you're not here. If Maurice starts asking you questions he'll be here all night.
Sarah (*looking at Anna again*) Are you sure, Jack?
Jack I'll let you know if there's anything you can do. I promise.

Sarah hesitates, then exits with Jack

Long pause

Anna stirs, finally rising from the sofa. She takes stock of her surroundings then moves slowly, somewhat nervously, towards the hall

Pause

Jack returns. He immediately takes her in his arms, kissing her, holding her close to him

Anna Well—was it a good performance?
Jack (*still holding her*) Almost as good as the one you gave on the telephone this afternoon. I can't say more than that, Anna!

Anna gives an uneasy little laugh as Jack releases her. At that moment the front door bell rings. They both turn and look towards the hall

(*Quietly; yet unable to conceal a note of tension*) That's the doctor!

Anna makes a sudden movement towards the sun-lounge. Jack restrains her

Wait! I don't want you to go, not yet!

Jack takes hold of Anna's arm and leads her towards the door of the study

Stay in here, Anna, until I call you. (*He opens the door*)

As Anna hesitates

It's all right, Anna! Please do as I say! Please, darling!

Anna exits into the study

Jack closes the door and moves back to the sofa. He quickly collects the rug and cushions and returns them to the sun-lounge. The door bell rings again.

Jack turns, surveys the room, and after a final glance at the sofa goes out into the hall

Pause

The front door opens and closes and voices are heard, off

Jack enters with Dr Maurice Young. Maurice, a middle-aged GP, is not at all happy at having to make yet another house call. He carries a bag

Jack It's good of you to turn out at this time of night, Maurice. I appreciate it.

Maurice Yes, well—you know what they say. "Duty must be done—the rule applies to everyone." Except that it doesn't of course. You try and get hold of a plumber at this time of night!

Jack You're talking about the élite! Now let me get you a drink.

Maurice No. Not for me, thank you.

Jack Are you sure?

Maurice Quite sure. (*He looks at his watch*) I take it—I'm here because of Sarah?

Jack Yes, I'm worried about her. Very worried. I just don't know what to do, Maurice.

Maurice (*a trifle wearily*) There's no need for you to be unduly worried. I've already told you that. The time for you to get worried, my dear chap, is when I'm worried. And I'm not a bit concerned about her at the moment. She's depressed, and a little overwrought perhaps, because of what happened to her brother, but that's understandable. Just give her time.

Jack (*stopping him*) Maurice, forgive me. This is no reflection on you, please don't think that, but—in my opinion she's worse, a great deal worse than when you first saw her.

Maurice What makes you think she's worse?

Jack Her fits of depression last longer and are more intense than they used to be . . .

Maurice Ah, yes—well . . .

Jack And now, she never stops talking about suicide.

Maurice You mean—she's threatened to commit suicide?

Jack (*after a calculated hesitation*) Well, no, not exactly. Although—I must admit there have been times when I've wondered whether. . . . One day last week I came home early. She was in the garden, standing by the pool, just staring at the water. There was a strange expression on her face, Maurice. It crossed my mind that. . . . The truth is, she's obsessed with the subject. She hardly ever talks about anything else.

Maurice Yes, well—again that's understandable in view of what she's been through. She was very fond of her brother.

Jack I know that . . .

Maurice You really must be patient. Give her time. (*He moves towards one of the chairs*)

Jack (*irritated*) I don't think it's a question of time. Not any longer. It's my opinion she's on the verge of—not just a nervous breakdown—but something far more serious.

Maurice (*sitting*) My dear fellow, I'm the doctor! Let me be the judge of that. You wouldn't consult me if you wanted to buy a house, now would you? (*He puts his bag down*)

Jack I'm sorry, Maurice, but I don't think you understand what's happened to Sarah. It's almost as if she's living in a world of her own. She constantly imagines things; all sorts of things . . .

Maurice (*barely concealing his impatience*) Yes, yes, you told me about her hearing the piano and being under the delusion . . .

Jack (*sharply*) I'm not talking about that!

Maurice looks at Jack, a shade surprised by his tone

Maurice Then what are you talking about?

Jack crosses to the chair and stands for a moment looking down at Maurice

Jack I'm talking about what happened last night. (*Pause*) She had a dream, I suppose you'd call it a nightmare. I had to wake her up. She dreamt I was involved in a car accident. That I'd knocked a girl down and that for some obscure reason, I was compelled to bring the girl back here. This morning, at breakfast, she made no reference to the dream and neither did I. Then suddenly, quite out of the blue, just as I was leaving for the office, she started talking about the girl—about the accident—as if it was for real. As if the incident had actually happened.

Maurice Didn't you tell her it was just a dream?

Jack Yes, of course I did! But she didn't believe me. She seemed convinced that I was in trouble—real trouble. But that's not all! She telephoned me this afternoon, at the office. It was most embarassing. She said she'd been giving the matter thought and felt sure the only thing for me to do was to go to the police and tell them the whole story.

Maurice What did you say?

Jack I didn't know what on earth to say. I knew the girl on the switchboard was listening. She listens to every damn thing. In the end I said, "All right, Sarah, my love, if that's what you want," and I rang off.

Maurice Has she mentioned the call since?

Jack No, but I've hardly seen her. I went straight from the office to The Grange. It was the Hoskins' house-warming. We were both supposed to go but Sarah can't bear the sight of Hoskins . . .

Maurice Who can?

Jack . . . and in any case she wasn't up to it.

Maurice nods. Pause. He appears to be giving Jack's story careful thought

Maurice Where is Sarah now?

Jack She's in her room. When I got back Kate Warren was here. Whether she sent for Kate I wouldn't know. It's possible. The moment Kate left Sarah complained of a headache and went to bed.

Maurice I see. Well—I'd better take a look at her. (*He rises and picks up his bag*)

Jack No—I'd rather you didn't, Maurice.

Maurice turns; a shade surprised

I finally persuaded her to take a dose of your medicine, so she's probably asleep by now. (*Suddenly; with a note of desperation*) What on earth are we going to do about Sarah? Believe me something must be done—and done quickly!

Maurice You'd like a second opinion, is that it?

Jack Yes. Frankly, I would.

Maurice (*a shade annoyed*) Is that why you sent for me, at this time of night?

Jack Yes, it is! I'm sorry Maurice, dragging you out like this, but I really do think it's about time we consulted someone else . . .

Pause

Maurice Well, in view of this new development, in view of what you've told me . . .

Jack Don't leave it, there's a good chap! Get on to it straight away. Please!

Maurice (*conjuring up a faint smile*) Very well. Tomorrow morning, first thing. I promise you.

They move towards the hall

Jack I play squash every now and then with a chap called Hilton-Reed. I don't know whether you know him?

Maurice I've met him. Tallish chap; has rooms in Wimpole Street.

Jack He's a psychiatrist.

Maurice Is he? Yes, well—we can do better than that. You must leave this with me. I'll deal with it.

Maurice exits

Jack slowly turns and moves down to the study. He stands deep in thought

Pause

The study door opens and Anna appears

Jack (*looking up*) Did you hear that?

Anna Yes ...

Jack All of it?

Anna (*softly*) Yes ...

Jack (*crossing to Anna*) Well, don't look so worried. Everything's going to be all right, I promise you. (*He watches her*) But I shall need your help, Anna. You realize that?

Anna Yes, I realize it. (*An uncertain pause*) It's still ... Thursday night ... ?

Jack Yes. Thursday night. (*He points to the patio door*) I want you here, by nine o'clock. Not a minute later.

Anna I'll be here, but ... (*She hesitates*)

Jack But, what?

Anna What about the housekeeper? What if she suddenly takes it into her head to come home early?

Jack I've told you about Lucy! It's her birthday. That's why I picked Thursday. She's going to a concert with some friends.

Anna But supposing the police don't believe your wife has committed suicide? What if they suspect ...

Jack Anna, my love, no one is going to suspect anything! The doctor will confirm my story about her state of mind, about the way she's been behaving during the past three months—so will Lucy and Kate Warren too, if necessary. There's absolutely nothing for you to worry about! (*He takes a tiny bottle out of his pocket*) Now, these pills you gave me. (*He looks at the pills*) You're sure, quite sure, they'll put her to sleep?

Anna Yes, I'm sure.

Jack For how long?

Anna Five or six hours, maybe longer.

Jack (*nodding*) Once we've got the nightdress on her it won't take us long to get her down to the pool.

Anna Why the nightdress? Is that necessary?

Jack Yes, it is.

Anna Why? I don't see why ...

Jack It's important, Anna! I want people to think she went down to the pool on the spur of the moment.

Jack takes hold of Anna and leads her into the sun-lounge. When they reach the patio door he switches off the lights and draws back the curtains

Now you know which way to go. As soon as you get past the studio you'll see the gate. Turn left when you get out of the gate and walk about fifty yards down the lane. That brings you to the corner. There's an empty cottage directly opposite with one of our "For Sale" boards outside— your car's in the drive. (*He looks at Anna for a moment, then takes her in his arms*) Now remember what I told you. You wait outside, on the patio, until I let you in. You understand?

Anna (*breaking away from him and giving a nervous little nod*) Yes, I understand.

Jack (*opening the patio door*) Nine o'clock, Anna! No later!

The Lights fade to Black-out

Scene 3

The same. The following morning

Maurice enters followed by Lucy. He crosses to the sofa and puts down the bag he is carrying

Lucy I'll tell Mrs Radford you're here, sir.
Maurice You say Mr Radford's already left for the office?
Lucy Yes, sir. He left some time ago. (*A slight hesitation; then:*) I'm afraid Mrs Radford's in a very bad way this morning, Doctor.
Maurice Yes, I know. She telephoned me.
Lucy Mr Radford's very worried about her. The poor man was quite beside himself when he left the house. I felt quite sorry for him.
Maurice Where is Mrs Radford now?
Lucy I imagine she's in her room. But I've seen very little of her this morning.
Maurice Didn't she come down to breakfast?
Lucy No, but that's not unusual. She very rarely does these days. It's usually a cup of coffee and a biscuit. In the middle of the morning.

Maurice gives her a little nod of dismissal, at the same time glancing at his watch. Lucy hesitates

Doctor, forgive me, but—may I ask you something?
Maurice Yes of course.
Lucy When a person commits suicide, like Mr Donnington ... (*she hesitates*)
Maurice Yes?
Lucy Is it possible ... I mean, is it very likely that another member of the family will. ... Well, what I'm trying to say ...
Maurice I think I know what you're trying to say, Lucy.
Lucy Mrs Radford's acting very strange these days. And I'm not the only one that's noticed it, Doctor.
Maurice Yes, well—there's no need for you to worry, Lucy. She'll soon be on the mend, I promise you. Only these things take time, unfortunately. Now perhaps you'll let Mrs Radford know I'm here.

Lucy turns toward the hall

Sarah enters

(*Brightly*) Good morning, Sarah.

Lucy exits

Sarah Thank you for coming, Maurice.
Maurice I was going to drop in anyway. I've made an appointment for you to see a specialist, Sarah. There's nothing for you to get alarmed about, my dear, but both Jack and I feel that. ... Anyway, I've arranged for you to see a Dr Trenchman. The appointment's for next Monday, three o'clock. I'll let you have the address later.

Sarah What is Dr Trenchman—a psychiatrist?

Maurice Well—sort of, my dear. But don't worry about that. (*He smiles*) He's very clever and he's a charmer, which is much more important. You'll like him.

A slight pause. Maurice looks at Sarah who stands nervously fingering a pendant on the necklace she is wearing

You sounded worried on the phone, Sarah.

Sarah (*with a note of tenseness in her voice*) Maurice, I sent for you because . . . I want you to tell me exactly what happened last night . . .

Maurice Last night?

Sarah Yes. Who did you see when you arrived here?

Maurice (*puzzled*) Who did I see?

Sarah Yes.

Maurice I saw Jack.

Sarah Just Jack?

Maurice Yes.

Sarah No one else?

Maurice No.

Sarah (*perturbed*) There was no one else here?

Maurice I've just said there wasn't.

Sarah Surely there was a girl. You must have seen her. (*She points*) She was lying on the sofa.

Maurice I saw no girl. I saw no one other than your husband.

Sarah slowly turns away from him. There is a strange, worried look in her eyes

Pause

(*Cautiously*) Tell me about this girl.

Sarah Jack went to the Hoskins'. It was their house-warming party . . .

Maurice I know. He told me.

Sarah On the way home a girl ran in front of his car and was knocked down. Jack was frightened. He daren't report the accident because he'd had rather a lot to drink—so he telephoned you, Maurice, and brought the girl back here.

Maurice (*gently*) I'm sorry, but that's not true. Jack sent for me last night because he was worried about you and he wanted me to get a second opinion. There was no other reason.

Sarah shakes her head

I assure you, Sarah—when I arrived there was no one here, other than Jack

Sarah I just can't believe that!

Maurice It's true. (*Pause*) What does Jack have to say about this?

Sarah He says the girl was just a figment of my imagination, part of a dream I had . . .

Maurice (*after a moment's consideration*) Yes, well—I didn't intend to tell you this, but. . . . That was one of the things we talked about last night. Your dream.

Sarah But I don't remember having such a dream! I don't remember anything about it.

Maurice (*softly*) Don't you, my dear?

Sarah Maurice, I saw the girl! She was here!

Pause

Maurice Sarah, I want you to do something for me. Try and put this imaginary incident out of your mind. Try and forget all about it until your appointment on Monday. Now will you do that? Please ...

Sarah I'll try. I'll try, Maurice.

Maurice Dr Trenchman will help you. I'm sure he will. You'll feel quite different in a few weeks' time. Take my word for it. Meanwhile, if you feel that you'd like to see me, between now and Monday—if it's only for a chat—don't hesitate, just give me a ring.

Sarah (*fatalistically*) Thank you, Maurice.

Maurice (*picking up his bag and smiling at her*) Now, remember that. . . . (*He watches her for a few seconds*)

Maurice exits

Sarah moves down to one of the armchairs, a dazed, confused expression on her face. She sits in the chair, staring into space, nervously fingering the pendant again

Pause

Lucy enters carrying a duster

Lucy The dry cleaners have returned Mr Radford's blazer. I've put it on the bed.

Sarah says nothing

Can I get you some coffee, Mrs Radford?

Sarah shakes her head

Lucy Are you sure?

Sarah I'm quite sure.

Lucy rearranges the cushions, tidies the sofa and—moving behind Sarah's chair—crosses to the drinks cabinet. She busies herself at the cabinet

Long pause

Lucy (*noticing the glass of brandy*) Did you pour this, Madam?

Sarah (*not turning*) What?

Lucy Did you pour this?

Sarah (*her thoughts elsewhere*) I haven't poured anything.

Lucy Then it must have been Mr Radford. (*She continues dusting the cabinet, finally sorting out the various bottles. Then she looks at the glass again, picks it up and sniffs it*) It's brandy. What shall I do with it?

Sarah What?

Lucy It's brandy. What would you like me to do with it?

Sarah turns, looks at Lucy, then rises. She crosses to the cabinet and takes the brandy out of Lucy's hand. She stands quite still, staring at the glass. The significance of the brandy very slowly dawning on her

What is it, Madam?

Sarah Nothing. . . . Nothing, Lucy . . .

Lucy (*curiously*) Are you feeling all right? Can I get you anything?

Sarah No. Just . . . leave me, Lucy. I'm perfectly all right . . .

Lucy stares at her, then exits

Sarah, still holding the glass of brandy, moves down to the sofa. She stands looking at the cushions — then, deep in thought, she returns to the cabinet and puts down the glass. She is distinctly perplexed, her thoughts on the events of the previous evening

Lucy enters

Lucy Mr Curtis is here, Madam.

Sarah Mr Curtis? What does he want?

Lucy I don't know. He didn't say . . .

Sarah I don't wish to see anyone. Tell him. . . . No, no, wait a minute. (*She hesitates; then*) Ask him to come in. . . .

Lucy Are you sure? I can easily get rid of him . . .

Sarah No, I'll see him, Lucy.

Lucy exits

Sarah looks at the glass of brandy again, then moves towards the hall

Pause

Geoffrey enters

Geoffrey Thank you for seeing me, Mrs Radford — and forgive my dropping in like this. I'd have telephoned you but unfortunately . . .

Sarah That's all right, Geoffrey. But Jack's not here, I'm afraid. He's at the office.

Geoffrey Yes, I know. It's you I wanted to see. I'm leaving Donnington's, Mrs Radford — in fact I've already left, and I just wanted to say . . .

Sarah (*surprised*) You're leaving Donnington's?

Geoffrey Yes, and I just wanted to say goodbye to you, and to thank you very much for — well — so many things.

Sarah That's very kind of you, Geoffrey. But — this is a surprise! Jack never told me you were leaving. What are you going to do? Start up on your own?

Geoffrey That's what I'd like to do. If I could get the money from someone I'd do it like a shot, but my bank manager says it's just not on at the moment. In fact I'm overdrawn already. Anyway, I've landed a job in London. (*He adjusts his glasses*) At least, I think — I hope — I have.

Sarah I'm amazed. I never thought you'd leave Donnington's. How long have you been with us? It must be ten years at least.

Geoffrey It's over ten. I joined the firm the year your mother died.

Sarah That's right, you did! I remember.

Geoffrey I was very nearly a wide boy in those days. If I hadn't met your father when I did I don't know what would have become of me. I shall always be grateful to him, Mrs Radford. He knocked some sense into me—which was more than anyone else had been able to do.

Slight pause

Sarah Why are you leaving us? Is it because of Jack?

Silence

Have you had a row with him?

Geoffrey Well—yes . . .

Sarah You've never really got on with Jack, have you?

Geoffrey No, I haven't. I think he's always resented the fact that your father started me in the business and . . . well, I suppose there's been faults on both sides.

Sarah Tell me what happened? (*A moment*) I'd like to know. Please tell me . . .

Geoffrey Donnington's are involved in several projects outside of the UK—mostly in Spain. Jack handles that side of the business himself and he's very, very cagey about it. No one in the office seems to know quite what's going on. Yesterday morning—and purely by accident, I assure you—I opened a letter which was addressed to Jack and marked "Personal". It was from a man called Montserrat and referred to . . .

Sarah Montserrat?

Geoffrey Yes.

Sarah Are you sure that was the name?

Geoffrey (*surprised by the question*) Yes, I'm quite sure. Charles Montserrat. Why? Have you heard the name before.

Sarah avoids looking at him; she shakes her head

It had something to do with a time-sharing property in Malaga. I showed Jack the letter and naturally apologized for opening it. Knowing Jack I expected him to be put out of course, but he was furious! He very nearly went berserk! In the end I just couldn't take any more of his abuse. I collected my things and walked out.

Sarah (*her thoughts elsewhere*) I see.

Geoffrey (*studying Sarah*) I'm sorry this happened, Mrs Radford, because Jack's got a lot going for him. He's pulled off some fantastic deals.

Sarah Yes, I know. (*Suddenly; dismissing her thoughts and once again giving Geoffrey her attention*) Sit down, Geoffrey. Let me get you some coffee.

Geoffrey No, thank you, Mrs Radford. I'm on my way to London. I'm hoping to catch the ten-thirty.

Sarah You've plenty of time. And Sarah, please! I'm getting a little tired of Mrs Radford.

Geoffrey moves down to the sofa. There is a slightly uncomfortable pause

Geoffrey Sarah, now that I've left Donnington's, there's something I feel I ought to tell you. Maybe I should have told you this before now, but to be honest, I heard that you were not well and I didn't want to ... (*he hesitates*)

Sarah (*crossing to a chair near the sofa and sitting*) What is it?

Geoffrey is still hesitating

What is it you want to tell me?

Geoffrey About a fortnight before your brother died I went over to Seaford to take a look at a property. On the way home I called in a café. Whilst I was waiting to be served I became conscious of two people in the next cubicle and I suddenly recognized Jack's voice. He was with a girl and they were talking about Donnington's.

Sarah (*softly*) Go on, Geoffrey.

Geoffrey Jack was explaining to the girl that although he ran the business he didn't own it, that it was in fact owned jointly by you and your brother. The girl was curious. She asked Jack what would happen to Donnington's, who would inherit the shares, if by any chance something unfortunate happened to you and Edward.

Sarah And what did Jack say?

Geoffrey He just laughed and said, "I get the lot, Anna. But that's too much to hope for, I'm afraid."

Sarah (*staring at him; stunned*) That's too much to hope for. ... Are you sure, that's what he said?

Geoffrey Yes, I'm quite sure.

Sarah You say—he called the girl Anna?

Geoffrey Yes. It could have been Ann, I suppose.

Sarah What else did you hear?

Geoffrey Nothing of importance. The waitress came and they left while I was being served.

Sarah What was the girl like? Can you remember?

Geoffrey Yes, of course. I've seen her since. She's fairly tall, dark, quite good-looking. In her late twenties, I should imagine. She works at Turnbull's the chemists. I called there with a prescription and she served me. She's in the dispensary.

Sarah You sure it's the same girl?

Geoffrey I'm positive. I—I only hope I've done the right thing in telling you this.

Sarah Yes, you have, and I'm very grateful. And please—don't mention this to anyone else. Not that you would.

Geoffrey No, of course not. I wouldn't dream of it. (*He rises*) I may not get the job in London, of course. In which case, I'll still be around.

Sarah (*getting up*) In which case, Geoffrey, I'll always be glad to see you.

Geoffrey (*looking at her, half smiling, pleased by her remark*) Thank you, Sarah. Well—I'll be off then ...

Geoffrey exits

Left alone, Sarah paces slowly around the room, fingering her necklace, using

*it as "worry beads". Suddenly she stops pacing and looks at the phone. She
hesitates, then crosses to the table and consults a private phone book, finally
dialling a number. She waits whilst the number rings at the other end*

Sarah (*on the phone*). . . . Is that Boston and Ridgeway? . . . Could I speak to
Mr Boston, please? . . . Mrs Radford . . . yes, that's right. . . . Thank you.
. . . (*Pause*) Arnold? . . . Yes, it is . . . I thought you'd say that! . . . It is, a
very long time . . . Arnold, I'm sorry to hear Irene's so ill . . . I didn't
realize it was serious. . . . Kate Warren told me . . . I know, I know, my
dear. . . . (*Pause*) Arnold, I'd like to see you. . . . Well, as soon as possible.
. . . I'd be grateful if you could. . . . Three o'clock this afternoon? . . . Yes,
that's fine. . . . Oh—Arnold. I know you don't see Jack these days, but if
by chance you should hear from him, I'd rather you didn't mention our
appointment. . . . What, my dear? . . . No, no, it's nothing like that. It's
just that I want to change my will . . .

The Lights fade to a Black-out

SCENE 4

The same. Thursday night

*Jack is sitting in an armchair. He is dealing with correspondence. There are
several letters, envelopes, bills, etc. on the arm of the chair together with a
stiletto paper knife. He picks up the knife and slits open the envelope he is
holding. He appears faintly amused by the contents but in reality his thoughts
are on a very tired-looking Sarah who is sitting on the sofa attempting to alter
the hem of a skirt. She is wearing the dress Kate commented on. They both
have drinks. Jack's is on the other arm of his chair and Sarah's glass, which is
nearly empty, is on a small table by the side of the sofa. Pause. Jack rises—
gathers up the letters, bills, knife, etc., and takes them over to the small table
facing the sofa. He returns to his chair. As he does so Sarah looks up as if to
say something, then she changes her mind and closes her eyes. She sits for quite
a little while with her eyes closed, then she slowly opens them and continues
sewing. Pause. Sarah puts the sewing down and picks up her glass; she stares
at it, undecided whether to finish her drink or not; finally she does so and
replaces her glass on the table. Jack looks across at her*

Jack You're very quiet, Sarah, my love.
Sarah (*not looking at him*) Am I?
Jack Is anything the matter?
Sarah (*coldly*) No. Nothing. I—I feel tired. I think I shall go to bed.
Jack You've been very quiet all evening. What is it? Are you annoyed with
me? (*Silence*) Well—are you?
Sarah (*staring at him; quietly*) Why didn't you tell me about Geoffrey?
Jack So that's what's troubling you! (*He rises and crosses to the sofa*)
Well—I suppose you were bound to find out about him sooner or later.
I'm sorry, Sarah. I know how you feel about Geoffrey, but—believe me, I
had no alternative. I had to fire him.

Sarah (*astounded*) Fire him?
Jack Yes.
Sarah But that's not what happened!
Jack Not what happened? What do you mean?
Sarah You didn't fire Geoffrey. You had a row with him because he opened
one of your letters by mistake.
Jack Sure I had a row with him! A blazing row! But that's not why he left
us. I sacked him. And if you want to know why I sacked him ...
(*Suddenly, he stares at her, apparently concerned*) Is something the matter,
Sarah? You look very pale ...
Sarah (*wearily*) I—I suddenly felt ...
Jack What is it?
Sarah I don't know. I feel very strange all of a sudden as if ... I feel terribly
tired, Jack. I—I can hardly keep my eyes open ...
Jack Can I get you anything?
Sarah No ... no, I don't think so. It'll pass, I expect ...

Pause. Jack looks at her for a moment then sits on the arm of the sofa

Jack (*curious*) How did you know about Geoffrey?
Sarah He came to see me.
Jack (*surprised*) Geoffrey did?
Sarah Yes.
Jack When?
Sarah (*finding it difficult to concentrate*) When?
Jack When did Geoffrey come to see you?
Sarah A couple of days ago. He said it was no use, he just couldn't work for
you any longer. He had to leave ...
Jack I see. (*Pause*) Is that all he told you?
Sarah Yes.
Jack Nothing else?
Sarah (*not looking at him*) No—why?

Slight pause

Jack I discovered he was. ... Oh, it doesn't matter ...
Sarah Tell me! What did you discover?
Jack Some other time ...
Sarah Tell me now! I want to know ...
Jack I found out that he was accepting backhanders from other agents,
taking business away from Donnington's, and deliberately robbing us of
our commission.
Sarah Geoffrey!
Jack Yes, Geoffrey.
Sarah I don't believe this! I just don't believe it!
Jack It's true. That's why I fired him, there was no other reason. The letter
had absolutely nothing to do with it. (*He rises*) Look, Sarah, we'll talk
about this some other time. Not now, you're far too tired. (*He picks up her
glass*) I'll get you another drink. Then I should go to bed if I were you.
Sarah (*staring at him oddly*) I—I don't want another drink.

Jack Just a nightcap. I'm having one. It'll make you feel better. (*He crosses to the drinks cabinet. He turns his back on Sarah and starts "fixing" her another drink*)

Sarah watches him, then she slowly rises and moves towards the hall. She suddenly feels overwhelmingly weary again and clutches the arm of the sofa to stop herself from falling. There is a tense pause

Although he still has his back towards his wife Jack is quietly aware of what is happening. Sarah stands quite still, her eyes closed—then with a deliberate effort she turns and sinks back onto the sofa. Another pause. Jack has finished at the cabinet and brings the drink down to Sarah who is now asleep. He stands staring at her. A long pause

(*Softly, testing her awareness*) Sarah, here's your drink.

There is no reply

Sarah . . .

Silence

Sarah, my love.

Pause. He puts the drink down on the table near the sofa, glances at his watch, then with his eyes still on Sarah, crosses to the phone and dials

(*On the phone; friendly*) . . . Kate? It's Jack . . . Katie, I wondered if you could drop in and see Sarah some time tomorrow? . . . She's frightfully depressed and unfortunately I'm spending tonight in London. . . . That's very sweet of you, I appreciate it. . . . I should be back some time in the afternoon . . . No, no, don't ring her. I don't want her to think I've been in touch with you. . . . What's that, my dear? . . . It's difficult to say, I think perhaps she's worried about seeing the specialist, she's been talking about it most of the evening. . . . Thank you, Katie. . . . Goodnight, my dear . . . (*He replaces the receiver*)

From now on Jack's manner becomes increasingly tense. He crosses into the sun-lounge, draws back the curtains, opens the patio door, and looks out into the garden. A pause—then he partly closes the door, and, obviously annoyed, returns to the sofa. He stands looking down at Sarah, then

Jack exits to the hall

Pause. From another part of the house a clock can be heard chiming the hour. Nine o'clock. Sarah stirs, as if she has heard the clock striking, then moving her body into a more comfortable position goes back to sleep. Another pause

Jack enters, carrying a nightdress

He puts the nightdress down, glances at Sarah, then returns to the sun-lounge. Once again he looks out into the garden. There is still no sign of Anna

(*To himself; angrily*) Anna, for God's sake, where are you? . . .

A pause—then, just managing to control his annoyance, he crosses and picks up the nightdress. As he moves cautiously towards Sarah

The Lights slowly fade to a Black-out

SCENE 5

The same. Friday morning. It is about 10.30. The door into the sun-lounge is partly open

Lucy is sitting on the sofa clutching a handkerchief. She is very distressed and is obviously a little frightened of Cliff Jordan who stands quietly looking down at her

Cliff ... Believe me, I've no wish to upset you, Mrs Baker. You've had a very distressing experience. But it's necessary that I ask you these questions.

Lucy (*in tears*) But you keep asking me the same questions over and over again!

Cliff (*smiling*) Only because you keep contradicting yourself.

Lucy Yes, I know. I'm sorry, Superintendent, but I'm so upset.

Cliff I appreciate that. Now supposing you tell me once again exactly what you did when you got up this morning?

Lucy I went across to the studio.

Cliff That's the building on the other side of the swimming-pool?

Lucy Yes. I went to collect a vacuum cleaner. I left it there yesterday afternoon.

Cliff I see. Go on ...

Lucy The vacuum was quite heavy and on the way back to the house I stopped for a moment by the pool and that's ... when I saw ... (*tears again*) I—I just couldn't believe my eyes ...

Pause

Cliff How long were you in the studio?

Lucy About ten minutes.

Cliff You said twenty minutes the last time I asked you that question.

Lucy Did I? It—it may have been twenty minutes. I don't know. I didn't intend to stay there at all, I just meant to pick up the vacuum, but the room looked so untidy ...

Cliff I thought you said the room had been cleaned the day before?

Lucy Yes, it had, but—it still looked untidy. (*She continues crying; using her handkerchief*)

Cliff (*pleasantly*) I can see you're a perfectionist, Mrs Baker. Never satisfied.

Lucy Yes, sir.

A moment

Cliff When do you normally get up of a morning?

Lucy I'm usually dressed and downstairs by half past seven.
Cliff But this morning you were much earlier?
Lucy Yes, it was just gone half past six.
Cliff Why were you so early this morning? You were very late going to bed.
Lucy I was hoping to have the weekend off. I thought if I started early I'd be finished by two o'clock.
Cliff I see. Now tell me about last night.
Lucy Last night?
Cliff I understand you spent the evening in Brighton?
Lucy Yes.
Cliff What time did you get back?
Lucy I caught the last train. Only just, I'm afraid. I got home about one o'clock ...
Cliff And went straight to bed?
Lucy Yes.
Cliff You saw no one?

Lucy shakes her head

No one at all?
Lucy No ...

Cliff studies her for a moment or two, then:

Cliff (*dismissing her*) Thank you, Mrs Baker.
Lucy (*surprised*) May I go?
Cliff Yes, you may go.

Lucy rises

And if I were you I'd make myself a nice, strong cup of tea.
Lucy Yes, sir.

Lucy exits

Cliff looks around the room, quietly taking stock. He is attracted to the wall of books and moves closer in order to read the titles. He stands for a moment peering at the books, obviously very interested in them. He is reaching for one of the volumes when ...

Geoffrey enters from the sun-lounge

Cliff turns and stares at him

Geoffrey (*tensely*) Superintendent Jordan?
Cliff (*moving towards him*) Yes?
Geoffrey My name's Curtis. I'm a friend—was a friend of Mrs Radford's.
Cliff What can I do for you, Mr Curtis?
Geoffrey (*clearing his throat*) I've just heard about Mrs Radford and ... I don't know what conclusion you've come to, Superintendent ...
Cliff (*studying him*) I haven't come to any conclusion, not yet.
Geoffrey Well, I have! I don't believe that Sarah—Mrs Radford—did commit suicide!

Cliff (*politely*) You don't?

Geoffrey No, I don't. (*A slight hesitation*) I think she was murdered.

Cliff Do you? Now that's interesting. I'm glad you dropped in, Mr Curtis. Sit down.

Geoffrey hesitates, then sits in one of the armchairs. Cliff perches himself on the arm of the sofa, facing him

What makes you think Mrs Radford was murdered?

Geoffrey I was with her only yesterday afternoon and she was perfectly normal, not in any way perturbed. (*Almost angrily*) She didn't take her own life. Believe me she didn't!

Cliff You were with her yesterday afternoon?

Geoffrey Yes. We had tea together.

Cliff Here?

Geoffrey No, in the village. Perhaps I'd better explain . . .

Cliff It might be a good idea, sir.

Geoffrey Until quite recently I worked for Donnington's. That's an estate agents that Mrs Radford . . .

Cliff I know the firm.

Geoffrey I left Donnington's and applied for a job in London. Unfortunately I didn't get it. Sarah—Mrs Radford—knew about my application, I'd already discussed it with her, and she very kindly asked me to . . . keep her informed.

Cliff Which is why you had tea together?

Geoffrey (*a shade uncomfortable*) Yes, I telephoned her and she suggested we . . . met in the village.

There is a pause. Cliff is weighing Geoffrey up

Cliff You say, you worked for Donnington's?

Geoffrey Yes, I was with them for ten years.

Cliff Tell me a little bit about the firm. Who exactly runs it?

Geoffrey The business originally belonged to Mrs Radford's father. When he died he left it lock, stock and barrel to Sarah and her brother Edward. Shortly afterwards Sarah married Jack Radford. Jack's been running the business ever since.

Cliff I see.

Geoffrey Unfortunately Edward Donnington committed suicide. You must have read about it. It was in all the papers.

Cliff Yes, I read about it. It was very sad. He was a marvellous pianist.

Geoffrey Sad, yes. But it was a lucky break for Jack Radford.

Cliff (*quietly*) Why do you say that, sir?

Geoffrey Jack didn't get on with Edward. Edward, quite rightly in my opinion, didn't trust him. Also—I shouldn't say this, I know, but—Jack knew that while his brother-in-law was alive he'd never get complete control of Donnington's. Which is what he's been after all these years.

Cliff rises, then looks quietly down at Geoffrey

Cliff (*slowly*) Let's get this quite clear. It's your opinion that Mrs Radford didn't kill herself and that she was in fact murdered ...
Geoffrey Yes ...
Cliff ... by her husband?
Geoffrey I—I didn't say that!
Cliff Not in so many words, perhaps.
Geoffrey (*rising*) It's for you to decide who committed the murder, Superintendent. But murder it was, I'm in no doubt about that!

Slight pause

Cliff May I ask you a personal question, sir?

Silence

Did you leave Donnington's on your own accord? Or did you—to put it bluntly—get the bullet?
Geoffrey (*obviously resenting the question*) I had a flaming row with Jack Radford and walked out. I wouldn't call that getting the bullet would you?
Cliff No, I wouldn't.
Geoffrey In any case, my leaving Donnington's has got nothing whatsoever to do with what happened to Mrs Radford.
Cliff I agree. I couldn't agree more, sir.
Geoffrey Then why did you ask the question?
Cliff I had a reason, Mr Curtis. A very good reason. Let's leave it at that.
Geoffrey I'm sorry, that's just not good enough.
Cliff Not good enough?
Geoffrey No! I answered your question, so I've every right to know why you ... (*He freezes; stunned*)

Sarah enters from the hall

Geoffrey stares at her in amazement

Sarah!

Sarah looks tense; overwrought. There are signs of tears

Sarah Hallo, Geoffrey. It was very kind of you to come.
Geoffrey (*bewildered*) But I thought ... I thought you were ... (*He turns towards Cliff in utter bewilderment*)
Cliff (*ignoring Geoffrey*) Are you feeling better now, Mrs Radford?
Sarah Yes, I am, thank you. I'm sorry I had to go and lie down, but—I felt so awful. It won't happen again, I promise you.
Geoffrey (*to Cliff*) I don't understand! What happened here this morning?
Sarah (*staring at him*) What happened? Don't you know?
Geoffrey I bumped into a cousin of mine, the one that runs the Beauty Parlour. She said she'd just been told that you'd ... committed suicide ...
Sarah That I'd committed suicide? ...
Geoffrey Yes. But—WHAT DID HAPPEN?

A moment, then:

Sarah Jack's dead. His body was found by the pool, early this morning.
Geoffrey Jack!
Cliff He was murdered, Mr Curtis.

Geoffrey stares at Cliff, incredulously—then as the Lights fade he turns towards Sarah

CURTAIN

ACT II

SCENE 1

The same. The action is continuous

As the CURTAIN *rises, Geoffrey moves away from Sarah and, still bewildered, stares at Cliff*

Cliff Mr Radford's body was discovered by Mrs Baker, the housekeeper. It was by the pool. He'd been knifed.
Geoffrey Knifed?
Cliff Stabbed to death, Mr Curtis.
Geoffrey Good God! But—who did it? Who killed him?

Cliff looks at Geoffrey and shakes his head

And why the devil didn't you tell me about this? Why did you let me go on talking about Mrs Radford when all the time you knew perfectly well that she was alive?
Cliff (*quietly*) Don't you know why?
Geoffrey No, I don't.
Cliff I should have thought it was obvious. (*Dismissing him*) But we'll talk about that some other time.

Geoffrey is about to retort, then thinks better of it, and turns towards Sarah

Geoffrey If I can do anything for you, Sarah. If I can help in any way. . . . In any way at all, please let me know.
Sarah That's very kind of you, Geoffrey.
Geoffrey I shall be in Eastbourne most of today. I'm seeing some property people, but I shall be back by four o'clock.
Sarah Have they offered you a job?
Geoffrey Not yet, but I think they're going to.
Sarah Well—please don't commit yourself. Not until we've had a chance to talk things over.
Geoffrey (*hesitantly*) Very well . . .
Sarah You know so much about Donnington's.
Geoffrey I understand, Sarah. I won't do anything, not at the moment.

Geoffrey looks at Cliff again, hesitates, then exits through the sun-lounge

Slight pause

Cliff has taken a jotter pad out of his pocket and is studying notes he made during a previous interview with Sarah

Cliff Now that you feel better, do you think we could start again? (*He looks at the pad*) You were telling me about last night. . . . But, please, do sit down . . .

Sarah crosses to the sofa. Cliff watches her; he realizes that she is under a tremendous strain

You said something about your husband having an appointment in London. I believe you told me he was due to meet someone there this morning?
Sarah Yes, that's right.
Cliff Who was he due to meet, Mrs Radford?
Sarah I'm afraid I don't know. Jack didn't tell me.
Cliff He didn't tell you? Was that unusual? (*He moves nearer the sofa and stands looking down at her*)
Sarah No, not really. He hardly ever discussed his business arrangements with me.
Cliff I see. As I understand it, after dinner you had a few drinks, and your husband then went upstairs to collect his overnight case.
Sarah Yes.
Cliff Then what happened?

Sarah hesitates, it is almost as if she is trying to decide whether to confide in him or not

Sarah After about ten minutes he came downstairs with the suitcase . . . I was half asleep . . . he said something like "If I were you I'd go to bed, Sarah"—then he kissed me and . . . went out into the hall. That was the last time I saw him . . . except for this morning.

Cliff's eyes are still on her; there is a tiny doubt in his mind as to whether she is telling the truth

Cliff Tell me about this morning.
Sarah I was in bed . . . it must have been about half past six . . . I heard Lucy's voice calling me. At first I didn't realize where the voice was coming from, I thought she was in her room. . . . Then, as I started to get out of bed, I heard footsteps and suddenly Lucy appeared, tears streaming down her face. The next thing I knew we were down by the pool . . . and there was Jack's body.

A moment, then:

Cliff Thank you, Mrs Radford. (*He takes his eyes off her and returns the pad to his pocket*) We found the suitcase. It was in your husband's car, in the garage. We think he put the case in the car and then probably saw someone in the garden and went to investigate. At least, that's one theory. (*Pause*) I know this is a very difficult question for you to answer, so please—take your time. Do you know—or do you think you know who killed your husband?

Pause

Sarah No.

Cliff You've absolutely no idea who committed this murder?

Sarah No, I haven't.

Cliff Have you any idea *why* it was committed?

Sarah (*not looking at him*) No, I . . . just can't imagine why anyone should . . . do such a thing . . .

Cliff Can you think of anyone—other than Geoffrey Curtis—who might perhaps have had a quarrel with Mr Radford?

Sarah No, I'm afraid I can't. (*Curiously*) But—who told you about the quarrel?

Cliff Mr Curtis did. He was quite frank about it.

Sarah Yes, well—I'm afraid squabbles are inevitable in a firm the size of Donnington's.

Cliff But I wouldn't have described Mr Curtis' row with your husband as being a "squabble" exactly. Would you? After all, Mr Curtis more or less lost his job over it. However—tell me about your friend Mrs Warren. How did she get on with Mr Radford?

Sarah (*totally surprised by the question*) Katie Warren?

Cliff Yes.

Sarah (*rising*) They were very good friends. But—why are you interested in Mrs Warren?

Cliff I'm interested in her because, as I understand it, there was a time when Mrs Warren wasn't exactly on friendly terms with either you or your husband.

Sarah (*a shade annoyed*) What are you suggesting? That Mrs Warren killed my husband because of an unfortunate car accident that happened eighteen months ago.

Cliff An accident in which her teenage daughter was killed. No, I'm not suggesting that. I'm simply looking for a motive, Mrs Radford. However remote.

Sarah (*relentless*) Yes, well, to be absolutely truthful, Kate—Mrs Warren— did blame Jack at first. For almost a year in fact she refused to speak to either of us. Then one day I bumped into her in Worthing and after a flood of tears I finally convinced her that the accident wasn't his fault. Since when, I'm glad to say, the three of us have been the best of friends.

Cliff Thank you. That's what I wanted to know. (*Friendly*) Incidentally, I understand the accident happened quite near where I now live. Croxley Bridge.

Sarah It happened on the bridge.

Cliff *On* the bridge?

Sarah Yes. There was a lorry that should have given way. Jack slammed his brakes on and, for some unaccountable reason, they failed to work. The car went over the parapet and into the river. Caroline, poor girl, was trapped.

Cliff But your husband escaped, uninjured?

Sarah stares at him for a moment, then rises

Sarah (*quietly*) Yes. He was lucky.

Cliff (*casually*) What was Miss Warren doing in the car?

Sarah My husband was driving back from London. He saw Caroline standing at a bus stop and offered her a lift.

Cliff Then it's not true that they'd spent the evening together in London?

Sarah No, it's not true! That was just a nasty little rumour!

Lucy enters; she is holding a cup of tea in her hand

Lucy (*to Sarah*) Excuse me—but there's a Mr Boston to see you. He say's you're expecting him.

Sarah Oh, dear! Yes, of course! I've an appointment with him. Where is he, Lucy?

Lucy Well, at the moment he's talking to the Sergeant.

Cliff Would that be Arnold Boston? Boston and Ridgeway?

Sarah Yes he's brought some papers for me to sign.

Cliff Do you still wish to see him?

Sarah (*hesitating*) I—I don't know. I don't know whether I'm up to seeing anyone at the moment.

Cliff I know Arnold Boston. He's by way of being a friend of mine. I'll have a word with him first.

Cliff exits

Lucy I've brought you a cup of tea.

Sarah shakes her head

Come along, it'll make you feel better!

Slight pause

Sarah (*taking the cup*) Very well. Thank you, Lucy.

Lucy How long will the police be here?

Sarah It's impossible to say.

Lucy They're searching for something, if you ask me. They're looking everywhere. (*She shakes her head; distressed*) I don't know what's happening to this neighbourhood! I really don't! What with rape and robbery, it's quite terrifying. Only last week a shopkeeper was stabbed to death at Belton Green, practically on his own doorstep.

Sarah Yes, I know. I read about it ...

Lucy The police found the knife in a letter-box of all places.

Sarah Yes, Lucy ...

Lucy And then there was that poor soul who was raped. She was on her way back from the hairdressers, she'd just had a perm.

Sarah Yes, Lucy! Yes! I read all about it.

Lucy (*a moment; hesitating*) I—I was going to have the weekend off, Mrs Radford, but I'll ring my friend if you like and tell her I can't make it.

Sarah No, don't do that.

Lucy Are you sure? I'll stay if you like.

Sarah No, no! I'd like you to keep to your arrangements.

Lucy exits

Pause

Sarah stands staring at the cup she is holding. After a little while she crosses to the table and, putting down the cup, picks up the phone. She appears strained, a shade tense; it is obvious that she is in two minds about making a phone call. Eventually she decides not to do so and slowly replaces the receiver

    As she does so Arnold Boston enters from the hall. He carries a document case

Arnold . . .

Arnold Sarah! My dear! I'm so sorry (*He crosses to her and puts down his case*) When the police told me I. . . . At first, I just couldn't take it in, I couldn't believe it. (*He shakes his head*)

Sarah I know. I keep thinking it isn't true. That it hasn't happened.

Arnold (*after an awkward pause*) Sarah, I just don't know what to say to you . . . Jack and I were never very close, I'm afraid. Somehow we just didn't . . .

Sarah (*suddenly, but not unfriendly*) You didn't like Jack, did you Arnold?

Arnold (*a moment, then:*) I used to like him in the old days, but when your father died and he took control of Donnington's something happened to him. He was no longer the sort of person I felt I could do business with. (*He shrugs*) Maybe I was wrong. My junior partner never stops telling me I must move with the times. (*He looks at his document case; then decides not to open it*) Has Cliff been difficult? He can be sometimes.

Sarah Cliff?

Arnold Cliff Jordan.

Sarah looks at him, puzzled

The Superintendent.

Sarah Oh! No, on the contrary. He's been most considerate. I felt pretty awful when he started questioning me, but he insisted I rest for a little while. (*A moment*) Cliff Jordan? (*Thoughtfully*) Haven't I read something about him, quite recently?

Arnold It's more than likely. He's written a book. And a very good book it is. I'm told he's done rather well out of it. There's even been some talk of his leaving the Force on the strength of it. He's a very shrewd man, Sarah. So be careful, my dear.

Sarah (*puzzled*) Why should I be careful?

Arnold Why? Because it won't be long before he's asking me the all important question. "Why did Mrs Radford want to change her will?"

Sarah But—he doesn't know about the will! Or does he? Have you told him?

Arnold No, of course I haven't. But that's the point I'm making. He'll find out about it. (*Pause*) Incidentally, why did you change your will? You never told me.

Sarah I discovered, quite by accident, that Jack was having an affair with someone . . .

Arnold (*surprised*) Jack was . . . ?

Sarah Yes. With a girl called Anna Truman. She works at Turnbull's, the chemists.

Arnold Turnbull's? (*Thoughtfully*) I may know the girl, I'm constantly dropping into Turnbull's with my wife's prescriptions . . . (*A moment*) . . . Is she dark, attractive, quite tall . . . I should imagine about twenty-seven?

Sarah Yes . . .

Arnold (*a note of disbelief in his voice*) And you say Jack was having an affair with this girl?

Sarah nods

You're sure?

Sarah I'm quite sure.

Arnold Have you told the Superintendent about this?

Sarah No, I haven't.

Arnold Then you must do so at once! It's possible Miss—Truman, did you say her name was?—may be able to help the police. Besides which, if you don't tell them, and they suddenly find out that you knew about Jack, they might very easily suspect that you had something to do with the murder.

Sarah stares at Arnold, apparently surprised by his statement, then she moves away, partly turning her back on him. Arnold watches her, puzzled by her reaction

Would you like me to talk to Cliff? Would you like me to tell him about Miss Truman?

Sarah (*turning and facing him again*) No, I'll tell him. If you think it's necessary.

Arnold It is, Sarah. Very necessary, I assure you. (*He changes the subject; indicating his case*) We'll discuss this some other time. You won't want to talk about it now.

Sarah (*softly*) It's no longer important.

Arnold (*staring at her for a moment*) Give me a ring, my dear, if you need advice—or if you think I can be of help in any way.

Sarah Thank you, Arnold.

Arnold moves towards the hall

I was very sorry to hear about your wife. I hope she'll soon get better.

Arnold She won't, I'm afraid. She'll be an invalid for the rest of her life, unless a miracle happens.

Sarah I'm sorry, Arnold. Do give her my love.

Arnold (*after a faintly embarrassed hesitation*) You heard about it, of course? You know what happened?

As Sarah shakes her head

She went to Spain on holiday with a friend of hers. The apartment they were sharing—the whole building in fact—suddenly collapsed. Her friend was killed outright and Irene escaped with what they thought, at the time, were minor injuries. Unfortunately, they were wrong. (*Resignedly*)

Anyway—she's alive and she's not too depressed at the moment, which is something. I'm taking her to see a faith healer tonight. He's been recommended by a friend of mine. So we'll see, we'll see. . . . (*He gives a little nod*)

Arnold exits

On Arnold's departure, Sarah's manner changes. It is obvious that she is now not only worried but is very uncertain about something. It is almost as if she is struggling mentally; trying to reach a decision of importance. There is a tense pause as she stands by the sofa, her back to the hall, restlessly fingering her necklace

Cliff enters

Cliff Mr Boston said you wanted to see me.
Sarah (*turning; hesitant*) Yes, I'm afraid I owe you an apology, Mr Jordan.

Cliff looks at her. He makes no comment

I hope you'll forgive me. I've been stupid, very stupid, I'm afraid. I realize that now. (*An uncertain pause*) I didn't tell you the truth about . . . last night . . . about what happened here . . .
Cliff (*quietly*) Didn't you, Mrs Radford?
Sarah No, I'm sorry. I lied to you. I don't know why I lied to you. Maybe it was because I was frightened, maybe it was just because. . . . (*A shade distraught*) Since my brother died, I've been desperately worried. Quite ill in fact.
Cliff (*nodding*) I've had a talk to your doctor. He told me.
Sarah Yes, I know, but—what he wouldn't tell you was, for some time now I've suspected that Jack. . . . (*Again she hesitates, then:*) I suddenly found out that my husband was having an affair with a girl called Anna Truman. She works at a chemist's in Brighton. Turnbull's. At first I didn't know what to do about it. I thought of confronting my husband and having it out with him. Finally I telephoned Miss Truman and we agreed to meet without Jack knowing . . .
Cliff Go on, Mrs Radford . . .
Sarah Much to my surprise I took a liking to the girl. I really liked her. For one thing she was quite different from what I expected. Also it didn't take me long to realize that she was out of her depth and completely under Jack's influence. We sat in my car, just the two of us, talking. . . . We talked for hours, and in the end she broke down and told me . . . what I already suspected . . .
Cliff (*puzzled*) What you suspected?
Sarah Yes.
Cliff You mean—that she was having an affair with Mr Radford?

Tiny pause

Sarah Not just that.
Cliff (*still puzzled*) Not just that?
Sarah No.
Cliff Well—what else did she tell you?

Sarah She told me that my husband was going to kill me . . . that my body was going to be found in the swimming-pool and that it would look as if I'd committed suicide.

Cliff And you believed her?

Sarah I didn't know whether to believe her or not. It seemed incredible to me that Jack would do such a thing, and yet . . . strange things have been happening to me since Edward died, things I couldn't understand, just couldn't account for. . . . Some of my friends—even Dr Young—began to think I was going out of my mind . . .

Cliff (*slowly; moving down to her*) Mrs Radford, let me get this straight. I want to make quite sure I understand what you're saying. You were told, by Miss Truman, that your husband was going to murder you?

Sarah nods

And that he was going to fake the murder so that it looked like suicide?

Sarah Yes . . .

Cliff (*incredulously*) And Miss Truman was going to help your husband to do this?

Sarah Yes, but—she said she'd now come to her senses and didn't intend to go through with it. In the end I decided to find out whether she was telling the truth or not—and there was only one way I could find out.

Cliff But—how was your husband going to commit this murder? What exactly was going to happen to you?

Sarah He was going to put me to sleep with some pills. Then—when I was unconscious carry my body down to the pool . . .

Cliff But that's not what happened.

Sarah I know.

Cliff You mean—he, too, changed his mind?

Sarah No. Jack didn't change his mind . . .

Cliff (*firmly*) Then what did happen last night?

Pause

Sarah It was about a quarter to nine. I was in the kitchen, clearing up, when my husband suddenly appeared with a couple of drinks. I took the one he offered me and said I'd join him in two or three minutes' time. When I did I had the same glass in my hand but a different drink from the one he'd given me.

Cliff A different drink?

Sarah Yes. I sat on the sofa, picked up some sewing, and after talking about Geoffrey Curtis I began acting as if the drink was having an effect on me. Eventually . . . I pretended to fall asleep . . . (*A moment*) Although my eyes were closed I knew that Jack was watching me. After a little while he moved away from the sofa and I heard him telephoning Katie Warren . . .

Cliff Your husband telephoned Mrs Warren?

Sarah Yes.

Cliff Why?

Sarah He said he was spending the night in London and he was worried about me. He asked her to drop in and see me some time today.

Cliff Go on, Mrs Radford. . . .

Sarah After the phone call I heard him moving around the room . . . I lay quite still . . . I knew that at any moment he'd return to the sofa. . . . I was terrified, but I simply daren't move. . . . It was then that I realized that there was only one way—only one possible way—I could save my life. . . . I had to kill him!

Cliff (*a moment; stunned*) Are you telling me that you killed your husband, Mrs Radford?

Sarah Yes, I am! (*Seeing the look of disbelief on his face*) I killed him! I had to—I had no choice!

Tense pause

Cliff How did you kill your husband, Mrs Radford?

Sarah I stabbed him! I stabbed him with a knife which I'd hidden behind one of the cushions.

Cliff is staring at her; curious

Cliff (*quietly*) Have you told anyone else about this?

Sarah No.

Cliff You didn't discuss it with Mr Boston?

Sarah No, I didn't.

Pause

Cliff I'm the only one, in fact, that's heard your story?

Sarah Yes.

Pause

Cliff I don't want you to repeat what you've just told me, Mrs Radford. Not to anyone. You understand?

Sarah stares at Cliff. There is a long pause between then

Sarah Yes, I understand.

Pause

Cliff Now tell me about the knife.

Sarah The knife?

Cliff You say it was on the settee, concealed behind one of the cushions?

Sarah Yes. I'd planted it there earlier in the evening.

Cliff Before your husband came into the kitchen with the drink?

Sarah (*tensely*) Yes. I—I knew he was going to kill me, so I had to defend myself. There was nothing else I could do.

Cliff You could have gone to the police.

Sarah It was no use my going to the police. You'd have simply questioned my husband who would have told you about my so-called hallucinations. And Dr Young would certainly have confirmed his story.

A tiny pause—then Cliff gives a little nod, as if agreeing with her statement

Cliff What did you do with the knife, Mrs Radford, after you'd killed your husband?

Sarah I took it back into the kitchen, cleaned it with detergent, and replaced it in one of the drawers.

Sarah And then what did you do?

Sarah I went upstairs, packed the suitcase—took it down to the garage and put it in the boot of the car.

Cliff (*quietly; watching her*) And then?

Sarah I came in here and wrapped . . . my husband's body in a blanket. By this time I was frightened, terrified. I suddenly realized what I'd done, that I'd actually killed someone. Finally, after a drink, I pulled myself together and . . . started to drag my husband's body along the stone path towards the swimming pool . . .

Cliff (*incredulously*) Are you telling me that you dragged your husband's body out of this room and through the sun-lounge? . . .

Sarah (*nodding*) Yes . . .

Cliff To the spot near the pool, where your housekeeper found him?

Sarah (*almost defiantly*) Yes!

Cliff You did this on your own?

Sarah Yes, I did!

Cliff Then what happened, after you'd left your husband's body by the pool?

Sarah I sat in that chair over there for—it must have been the best part of three hours. Finally, I went upstairs, had a bath, and went to bed. (*A short silence, then:*) My husband wasn't just a cheat and a womanizer. Please don't think that! I could probably have come to terms with that situation. But he tried to make me commit suicide, and when that failed he deliberately, quite deliberately, set out to kill me. (*A moment, then:*) I did a terrible thing. I know that. But believe me, I don't regret it. I shall never regret. Never!

There is another silence between them

Cliff (*quietly*) Tell me again about the knife. What sort was it?

Sarah (*hesitantly*) What sort?

Cliff Yes.

Sarah It was a long, thin, carving knife.

Sarah And you say it was on the sofa, hidden behind one of the cushions?

Sarah Yes.

Cliff What did you do with the knife after you'd committed the murder?

Sarah I told you!

Cliff Please tell me again.

Sarah I took it into the kitchen . . .

Cliff Yes?

Sarah I took it into the kitchen, cleaned it, and put it back in the drawer. But I've already told you this!

Cliff You have. You have indeed. (*He moves nearer to her*) And now, perhaps you'll tell me something else? (*Tiny pause*) Why have you lied to me?

Sarah (*taken aback*) Lied to you? But—I haven't lied to you!

Cliff I think you have. I think you invented that story about the drink, about falling asleep, about hiding a knife behind one of the cushions. I just don't believe you dragged your husband's body out of this room, across the sun-lounge, and all the way to the swimming pool. I don't believe it, because I don't believe you did kill your husband!

Sarah (*her voice rising to a pitch of tension*) I did! I tell you I did! I've told you the truth! (*She turns away from him*) I did kill him!

Cliff watches her, then he slowly shakes his head

Cliff We found the murder weapon. We found it ten minutes ago. Whoever killed your husband dropped the knife in the letter-box at the end of the lane. It was still covered in blood.

Sarah turns, startled. She is staring at Cliff as . . .

The Lights fade to a Black-out

SCENE 2

The same. Friday evening

Kate is on the telephone talking to someone. She looks a shade irritated

Kate (*on the 'phone*) . . . I'm sorry, but it's just not possible. . . . My dear, if I could help you I would, you know that. . . . What do you mean important? Important to you, or important to me . . . ? Yes, well, it's just not on, I'm afraid. . . . (*Coldly*) That's what I said, darling, it's just not on! . . . I can't, I've got a very hectic week ahead of me and I'm leaving for Edinburgh on Sunday . . .

Voices are heard in the hall and Kate turns towards them

Look, I just can't talk any longer, Geoffrey . . . I'm sorry I can't help you . . . (*She replaces the receiver*)

Lucy shows in Cliff

Lucy It's the Superintendent, madam.

Lucy exits

Cliff moves down to Kate

Kate I'll tell Mrs Radford you're here, but she's not feeling too good at the moment. Dr Young's only just this minute left. (*She begins to move towards the hall*)

Cliff Yes, I know. I've been talking to him. It's you I wanted to see, Mrs Warren.

Kate (*stopping*) Me?

Cliff Yes.

Kate Why me?

Cliff I'd like to ask you one or two ...

Kate Routine questions?

Cliff I'll try very hard not to make them too routine, Mrs Warren. Do you happen to know a young man called Geoffrey Curtis?

Kate (*surprised*) Why, yes. I—I know Geoffrey.

Cliff How well do you know him? (*He studies Kate*)

Kate We live near each other and we ... play bridge occasionally. (*She is aware of Cliff studying her*) He works for Donnington's.

Cliff He did. Not any longer.

Kate Really? Are you sure? (*Intrigued*) That's very interesting.

Cliff Interesting, Mrs Warren?

Kate Yes. (*She indicates the phone*) I've just been talking to him. He's flat broke. He tried to borrow some money from me. You say he's left Donnington's?

Cliff Yes.

Kate What happened?

Cliff He had a row with Mr Radford.

Kate Did he? Did he indeed? Well, that doesn't surprise me. He and Jack never really hit it off.

Cliff Was Mr Radford a difficult person to get on with?

Kate He could be difficult at times. But then, we can all be difficult at times, can't we?

Cliff How did you get on with him? I know Mrs Radford's a good friend of yours but it doesn't always follow that ...

Kate She's my best friend. And what are we leading up to, Superintendent?

Cliff Leading up to?

Kate You know what I mean. You were about to question me about that wretched car accident. About my feelings towards Jack Radford when my daughter was killed.

Cliff (*faintly amused*) I wasn't leading up to anything, I assure you. But since you've mentioned the accident. What were your feelings?

Kate I was angry, of course. Bloody angry! I would willingly have killed him. But later I came to realize that—in spite of the rumours—Jack wasn't to blame for what happened. Not in any way.

Cliff Thank you, Mrs Warren.

Kate For what?

Cliff For being so frank with me.

Kate Oh, I'm always frank, Superintendent. I probably get more pleasure out of being frank with people than anything else. Incidentally, I've been meaning to congratulate you.

Cliff On what?

Kate Your book.

Cliff (*surprised*) Oh. You've read it?

Kate No, I'm afraid I haven't. But I saw the article in the local paper.

Cliff nods

That must have pleased you, it was very complimentary.

Cliff I'd have been more pleased if they'd got the title right.

Kate What is the title?
Cliff *A Possible Explanation.*
Kate And what did they call it?
Cliff *An Impossible Explanation.*
Kate (*laughing*) Is this your first novel?
Cliff It's not a novel. I've simply taken half a dozen famous murder cases. Cases which were never solved ...
Kate And you've solved them?
Cliff (*laughing*) Well—you think I have when you're reading the book.
Kate Have you ever thought of leaving the police and becoming a full-time writer?
Cliff I think of nothing else, Mrs Warren.

Kate smiles, looks at him for a moment, then moves towards the hall again.

Sarah enters. She is wearing a dressing-gown and looks tired

Kate Are you all right, Sarah?
Cliff Mrs Radford ...
Sarah Yes, I feel better now.
Kate You'll feel better still when you've had a meal.
Sarah I don't feel like eating. I really don't.
Kate Well, you're going to! The doctor insists—and so do I!

Kate exits

Sarah turns towards Cliff. From now on her manner becomes slightly more tense

Cliff We've found your husband's wallet, Mrs Radford. It was in a ditch behind the studio. Needless to say it was empty.

Sarah makes no comment

I understand your husband hated credit cards and paid cash for almost everything.
Sarah Yes, he did. He invariably had quite a lot of money in his wallet. Sometimes as much as six or seven hundred pounds.
Cliff As much as that? I see. (*He looks at her for a second*) I saw Miss Truman this afternoon and we had, to say the least, an interesting conversation. She admitted, quite frankly, that she'd been having an affair with your husband. She made no bones about it.

Sarah makes no comment

She also confirmed what you told me. That the two of you had had a meeting and that you'd spent the best part of two hours discussing her relationship with Mr Radford.

Silence from Sarah

But what she didn't confirm was your story about the sleeping pills and your husband's abortive attempt to kill you. (*A moment*) She said that was just your imagination ...

Sarah (*quietly*) Is that what you think, that it was just my imagination?

Pause

Cliff To be frank, Mrs Radford. I'm not sure.

Kate enters carrying a tray with legs bearing an elaborate meal and a slim vase holding a single rose

Kate The meal's ready, Sarah.

Pause

Cliff's eyes are still on Sarah

Cliff I hope you'll soon feel better.

He nods to Kate and exits

Sarah doesn't move. Kate releases the legs on the tray and places it in front of the sofa

Kate Come and sit down. . . . (*Pause*) Come and sit down, Sarah, please . . .
Sarah (*preoccupied with her thoughts*) I'm sorry . . . it's kind of you, Kate, but—I just don't feel like eating anything.
Kate This isn't anything! Now come along! You've got to eat!

A slight pause, then Sarah crosses down to the sofa. As she sits Kate puts the tray nearer to her

I'm going back to my place for a short while. If you haven't eaten everything on that tray by the time I return I shall be very very angry!

As Sarah is about to say something

Now please, darling! Do as I say . . .

Sarah stares at the tray, finally picking up a small piece of Melba toast

I shall be back in an hour.
Sarah There's no need. There really isn't. You must have a hundred and one things to attend to.
Kate I have, but you're the most important. We've got to get you well again Sarah. Now don't just nibble! Eat up!

Kate exits

After a little while Sarah makes a movement, as if she is about to rise from the sofa, then she changes her mind and relaxes, slowly eating the piece of toast. She looks less tense than in the scene with Cliff although it is difficult to tell what she is thinking. There is another pause. She finishes the toast and is about to pick up another piece when she notices the rose. She stares at the slim vase, and the rose, apparently amused by them

Sarah Dear Katie . . .

Sarah starts laughing. Her laughter slowly gains momentum; there is almost a touch of hysteria in the laughter when suddenly the front door bell is heard.

Her laughter ceases. She turns and looks towards the sound. Pause. The bell rings again. Another pause—then she rises and pushes the tray to one side

   Sarah exits to the hall

Pause. The front door is heard to open and close

Sarah (*off*) Hallo, Geoffrey!
Geoffrey (*off*) Good-evening, Sarah. Are you alone?
Sarah (*off*) Yes . . .
Geoffrey (*off*) May I come in?
Sarah (*off*) You are in, Geoffrey.

   Geoffrey enters, followed by Sarah. He has taken off his glasses and is nervously cleaning the lenses with a handkerchief

Geoffrey I've been waiting in the garden. I saw the Superintendent leave and Mrs Warren, but I wasn't sure whether you had anyone else with you.
Sarah Why wait outside, Geoffrey?
Geoffrey Well, I didn't want to disturb you. I wondered whether. . . . It's very good of you to see me, Sarah. I appreciate it. I know how you must be feeling. (*He notices the tray*) Have I interrupted your dinner?
Sarah No, no, don't worry. I wasn't very hungry. Would you like a drink?
Geoffrey I'd like one, but I don't know whether I should . . . I had that pain again this morning.
Sarah Oh, I'm sorry to hear that. Was it bad?
Geoffrey Yes, I'm afraid it was, rather . . . (*with a nervous little laugh*) The trouble is of course I scare very easily these days.
Sarah Considering the fright you had, I think you've been very brave.

A slightly uncomfortable pause

Geoffrey I saw those people in Eastbourne. The ones I told you about. They've made me a very good offer.
Sarah How good?
Geoffrey They—they've offered me almost twice as much as I've been getting.
Sarah Well, in that case I wouldn't want to stand in your way. Obviously I'd prefer that you stayed with Donnington's, but I realize of course . . .
Geoffrey No, no, you misunderstand me! I'm not going to accept their offer.
Sarah You're not?
Geoffrey No, I. . . . Oh, dear, I'm afraid I'm not very good at this sort of thing.
Sarah (*puzzled*) What sort of thing? What are you trying to say, Geoffrey?
Geoffrey (*moving nearer Sarah*) I wanted to talk to you about this last night, but . . . Do you remember Humphrey Wingate? He used to work for Donnington's.
Sarah (*with a little laugh*) Yes, of course I remember Humphrey.
Geoffrey He started an agency of his own about four years ago, in Devon. He's done awfully well. He's asked me to join him, in fact he's offered me a partnership.

Sarah That's very generous of him.

Geoffrey Yes, it is. The snag is—well, it's not really a snag, it's just that . . . he'd like me to take an interest, a financial interest that is, in the company. (*He adjusts his glasses*) That's understandable really, if I'm going to be a partner.

Sarah (*not convinced*) Yes, I suppose it is.

Slight pause

Geoffrey He's mentioned the figure of a hundred and twenty-five thousand pounds, but if I could raise a hundred or even seventy-five thousand, I'm sure he'd be happy.

Sarah But surely you can't raise that sort of money? Only the other day you said the bank had flatly refused to lend you . . .

Geoffrey (*stopping her; agitated*) Yes, I know! I know. I remember what I said, but . . . the situation's changed a little bit since then.

Sarah Oh? In what way?

Geoffrey hesitates again, then

Geoffrey Well—I think perhaps I'd better put my cards on the table.

Sarah If you have any cards, Geoffrey, please do.

Geoffrey I want you—or rather Donnington's—to lend me the seventy-five thousand.

Sarah (*staring at him*) Why should Donnington's lend you anything?

Geoffrey Why? (*A little hurt*) Sarah, I did work for them for ten years.

Sarah Yes, and you were well paid for it.

Geoffrey I appreciate that, on the other hand . . .

Sarah (*dismissing the subject*) Anyway, it's not for me to say whether Donnington's should lend you, or anyone else, seventy-five thousand pounds!

Geoffrey Not for you?

Sarah No . . .

Geoffrey But you own the company . . .

Sarah I may own the company, but . . . look, Geoffrey I suggest you talk to the accountants.

Geoffrey (*with a faint note of defiance in his voice*) I'd rather you talk to them, Sarah.

Sarah looks at him. It is almost as if she is seeing him for the first time

Sarah Have you, by any chance, something else on your mind?

Geoffrey Yes I have, I don't think you realized what I said a moment ago.

Sarah What did you say?

Geoffrey I said I wanted to talk to you about this last night.

Sarah Well?

Geoffrey I knew Jack had an appointment in London so I came here.

Sarah (*amazed*) You came here, last night?

Geoffrey Yes, I got as far as the garden and then . . . (*He hesitates*)

Sarah And then what?

Geoffrey I saw you.

Sarah Where did you see me?

Geoffrey By the pool ...

Sarah What time was this?

Geoffrey About half past nine.

Sarah What would I be doing by the pool at half past nine at night?

Geoffrey That's exactly what I asked myself, Sarah. And then I saw what you were doing. You were kneeling down by Jack's body, searching his pockets.

Pause

Sarah (*hardly audible*) What else did you see?

Geoffrey I watched you for two or three minutes. I nearly joined you, then I suddenly remembered the row I'd had with Jack and I decided it would be stupid of me—very stupid—to get involved in ... whatever was happening to him ...

Sarah You still haven't answered my question. What else did you see?

Geoffrey Nothing else. I was too scared to stay. This morning, however, curiosity got the better of me. So I came here and pretended I knew nothing about the murder.

Sarah contemplates him for several seconds

Sarah (*finally*) Why are you telling me this?

Geoffrey You asked if there was anything else on my mind.

Sarah That's quite right, I did. Well—thank you for putting some more of your cards on the table. It never occurred to me that you had so many.

Geoffrey I'm sorry. I don't know what you mean.

Sarah Don't you, Geoffrey? (*a pause. She studies him*) Your eyesight isn't very good, is it? It never has been.

Geoffrey No, it's not terribly good, but—what are you suggesting? That it wasn't you I saw?

Sarah Where were you standing when you thought you saw me?

Geoffrey Near the studio.

Sarah That's a good thirty or forty yards from the pool.

Geoffrey Yes, I suppose it is. (*Quietly shaking his head*) But I saw you, Sarah. I know it was you. I had my doubts at first but—I even recognized the dress you were wearing. (*Tiny pause*) Look, please don't get me wrong. I'm not suggesting you killed Jack. I don't know whether you did or didn't. It's possible you just stumbled across his body after someone else had killed him. In any case, it's no concern of mine. (*A moment*) I didn't like Jack. I hated him. Hated his guts! (*After a long pause*) Please think over what we've talked about. The loan, I mean. If Donnington's can help me I'd be more than grateful, you know that. If necessary of course it needn't be a loan. It could be a sort of ... kind of ... golden handshake. Give me a ring when you've spoken to the accountants.

Sarah stares back at him, cold and unfriendly

The Lights slowly fade to a Black-out

Scene 3

The same. The following morning. Noon

Kate is sitting in an armchair finishing a cup of coffee. She is wearing a dress which is a replica of the one previously worn by Sarah. After a little while she looks towards the hall, rises, and puts down her cup

Maurice enters. He carries his bag and a morning newspaper

Kate How is she? How does she seem?

Maurice I've never seen her quite like this before. One minute she's quiet and subdued, her thoughts miles away, the next minute she's tense and argumentative. She even rambled on about the dress you're wearing. At one stage it did cross my mind that perhaps she'd been. . . . But that's absurd at this time of the morning!

Kate What were you going to say?

Maurice I was going to say, it did cross my mind that she'd been drinking.

Kate (*slightly embarrassed*) She did have two large vodka and tonics, I'm afraid.

Maurice Before breakfast!

Kate She very rarely eats breakfast these days.

Maurice I do wish you'd told me earlier. Anyway, we'll just have to wait and see what Dr Trenchman makes of her.

Kate That's on Monday?

Maurice Yes—three o'clock. I'd very much like someone to go up to town with her, if possible. (*Hesitantly*) I was wondering if by any chance . . .

Kate I'm awfully sorry, Maurice, but I shall be in Edinburgh practically the whole of next week . . .

Maurice Oh—well, not to worry.

Kate I'm leaving first thing on Sunday morning . . .

Maurice Not to worry, my dear. We'll think of something. (*He puts his bag down*) Tell me: how did she come to hear about this friend of hers?

Kate The local newspaper telephoned. Almost immediately afterwards she had a message from Donnington's. She was shaken, very badly shaken. Apparently she saw him last night. He came here.

Maurice Well, there you are. These things happen. Even to the young, I'm afraid. (*He looks at his watch*) I really must make a move. I was due at the hospital ages ago.

Kate Yes, and I'm due at the BBC.

Maurice Are you on the box tonight?

Kate Tomorrow night. We're rehearsing today.

Maurice My wife will be delighted. She loves your recipes. Personally, I don't think you can beat bacon and eggs.

Kate You can ruin bacon and eggs, too, Doctor.

Maurice How true! How very true . . .

Lucy enters

Lucy Excuse me, Mrs Warren. Mr Jordan's here. I understand Mrs Radford sent for him.

Kate gives Maurice a puzzled look

Kate When did she send for him, Lucy?
Lucy I don't know, Madam.
Kate All right. Ask him to come in.

Lucy exits

(*To Maurice*) I know nothing about this. Why should she want to see the Superintendent? (*She turns towards the hall, obviously mystified*)

Cliff enters

Cliff Good morning, Mrs Warren. Doctor . . .
Maurice Superintendent . . .
Cliff Mrs Radford telephoned me about half an hour ago. She said she'd like to see me as soon as possible.
Kate Did she say why?
Cliff No, she didn't.
Maurice She's had rather a nasty shock, I'm afraid. A friend of hers died last night.
Cliff (*nodding*) Yes. We know about Mr Curtis. The poor chap had a heart attack. (*He turns and looks at Kate*)
Kate I'll let Mrs Radford know you're here.

Kate exits

Cliff Doctor, the other day, when we were discussing Mrs Radford, you said her husband had been worried about her.
Maurice Yes. After Edward Donnington's suicide Jack was very concerned. I told you. She appeared to be suffering from delusions, hallucinations in fact.
Cliff Was that your diagnosis, or Mr Radford's?
Maurice (*crossing to one of the armchairs*) I'm not sure I know what you mean. (*He puts his bag down*)
Cliff (*after a slight hesitation*) We found a tape-recorder in the studio. It was hidden behind one of the cupboards. A very sophisticated machine. It even had a time mechanism fitted to it.
Maurice So? What are you suggesting?
Cliff I'm suggesting that maybe Mrs Radford did hear her brother playing the piano after all.
Maurice But that's nonsense!
Cliff Why is it nonsense?
Maurice Because the first time Sarah heard the piano—or thought she heard it—Jack was with her. And he most certainly didn't hear it!

Pause

Cliff What was your opinion of Jack Radford, Doctor? Your personal opinion, I mean. Did you like him?
Maurice Yes, I—er—I liked him.
Cliff What did you like about him?

Maurice He was a hard worker, he was devoted to his wife and he always
paid me in cash.

Cliff (*smiling*) You say he was devoted to his wife?

Maurice Very much so. Used to ring me up at all hours of the day and night
and just natter on about her.

Cliff Then obviously you'll be surprised to learn that he was having an
affair with someone.

Maurice Jack was?

Cliff Yes.

Maurice (*a moment, then:*) Well, no, not totally surprised. I learnt a long
time ago that devotion to one's wife doesn't necessarily rule out infidelity.
I have a patient who hates his wife, beats the hell out of her with
monotonous regularity. But I know for a fact that he's never slept with
another woman. His wife wishes to God he would. And so do I. (*He picks
up his bag*)

Cliff Has Mrs Radford ever consulted anyone else?

Maurice No, but I've arranged for her to see a Dr Trenchman. Her
appointment's for three o'clock on Monday.

Cliff Would that be Dr Ross Trenchman, Wimpole Street?

Maurice That's right. Do you know him?

Cliff I've met him. We both gave evidence in a Court case, about a year ago.
An extremely nice man.

Maurice Yes—and very clever. I only hope Mrs Radford keeps the appointment. I have a horrible feeling she might not do so. I was hoping Mrs
Warren would be able to go along with her but unfortunately she's away
for the week.

Cliff I sometimes wonder what Mrs Radford would do without Katie
Warren.

Maurice She's certainly been a great help just recently, there's no doubt
about that.

Cliff What happened to *Mr* Warren? You never hear of him these days.

Maurice He walked out on her a couple of Christmases ago. Couldn't take
any more of her cooking. At least, that's the story.

*Sarah enters. Her manner is odd; sometimes tense, sometimes vague and
distant. She carries a small bottle of capsules, given to her by the doctor*

Sarah Maurice—I thought you'd left.

Maurice I'm just off. (*He rises and picks up his bag*)

Cliff Good morning, Mrs Radford.

Sarah stares at Cliff

You asked me to call round. (*Pause*) You telephoned me.

*Sarah continues looking at him, finally she gives a little nod and turns her
attention to the capsules she is holding. Cliff glances at the doctor*

Sarah Maurice, these capsules . . .

Maurice Yes, Sarah?

Sarah What are they for?

Maurice I've just told you. Now stop worrying about them. Just take them. Take the first one tonight when you go to bed. Not before. And no more alcohol today, please.

Sarah No more alcohol?

Maurice That's right.

Sarah (*staring at the capsules*) You're sure about that?

Maurice I'm quite sure.

Sarah You're not just being bloody-minded?

Maurice No, I'm not.

Sarah You can be very bloody-minded at times. You know that, don't you Maurice?

Maurice Yes, my dear. And my patients never fail to remind me of the fact. Now you heard what I said? You mustn't drink. Not while you're taking the capsules. You understand, Sarah?

Sarah Yes, I understand.

Maurice That's important.

Sarah I understand, Maurice.

Maurice (*with a forced smile*) I'll drop in again tomorrow afternoon.

Maurice nods to Cliff and exits

Pause. Sarah stands looking at the capsules. Cliff watches her. After a moment she moves down to the desk, and with a slightly theatrical gesture, drops the bottle into the wastepaper basket

Cliff That's not very sensible, Mrs Radford.

Sarah (*vaguely*) No...?

Cliff No.

Pause

Sarah I'm afraid I don't feel very sensible this morning.

Cliff You should do what your doctor tells you. (*He goes to the wastepaper basket, retrieves the capsules and puts them on the desk*)

Pause

Why did you wish to see me?

Pause

Sarah You remember Geoffrey Curtis?

Cliff nods

He's dead.

Cliff Yes, I know. I'm sorry.

Sarah I'm not.

Cliff (*surprised*) You're not sorry he's dead?

Sarah No.

Pause

Cliff Why aren't you sorry?

Sarah He tried to blackmail me.
Cliff Mr Curtis did?
Sarah Yes.
Cliff When?

Sarah doesn't answer him

When did he try to blackmail you?
Sarah Last night. He came here, just after you left. At first he was very nice, very pleasant, then suddenly he turned nasty and started to blackmail me. He even threatened me . . .
Cliff Threatened you?
Sarah Yes, that's—when it happened. (*Quickly, tensely*) But it wasn't like Jack. Not the way I killed Jack. That was different. Quite different.
Cliff (*after an uncertain pause*) Tell me about last night, Mrs Radford.
Sarah Geoffrey tried to borrow money from me. When I refused he started talking about a golden handshake. Suddenly I lost my temper and . . . we had a terrible row. I grabbed hold of one of the table lamps and tried to hit him with it. While we were struggling he had a heart attack and died . . .
Cliff (*slowly; staring at her uneasily*) He had a heart attack and died? You mean—here, in this room?
Sarah Yes.

Pause

Cliff Then what happened?
Sarah I—I took him out to his car. Drove the car into a lay-by and left him there.
Cliff Did you, Mrs Radford?
Sarah Yes.
Cliff You left him in the car?
Sarah Yes, I've just said so!
Cliff Where did you leave him?
Sarah But I've just told you! In the lay-by!
Cliff Where was he sitting in the car?

She does not answer

Can't you remember? (*A moment; then:*) In the passenger seat?
Sarah He was in the passenger seat to start with, yes—but . . . I moved him. I had to move him because I . . . wanted people to think that . . . (*Her voice breaks*)
Cliff Mrs Radford, what you've just told me isn't true. Mr Curtis was seen driving his car into the lay-by. He was alone. A lorry driver saw him and spoke to him, only a few minutes before he died.
Sarah But he came here last night. We had a row. . . . He tried to blackmail me . . .
Cliff Geoffrey Curtis died in his car. He'd had a weak heart for some time and we know for a fact that it had been giving him trouble during the past

week or so. Believe me, you had absolutely nothing whatsoever to do with his death, Mrs Radford!

Sarah (*greatly disturbed*) Is this true? Are you telling me the truth?

Cliff Of course. Why should I lie to you?

Sarah But last night, the quarrel. ... Didn't it happen? Wasn't there a struggle ... ? Is it just my imagination? (*With a note of desperation in her voice*) Ever since Edward died, I've had these strange feelings. ... It's at night, when I'm alone, that I imagine things. Things that couldn't possibly happen to me ... and yet, the next day, the very next day, I'm convinced that ... they've taken place.

Cliff gives a sympathetic little nod

Cliff Yes, I know.

Sarah There are times when I'm not even sure about ... (*she hesitates*)

Cliff About what? (*Pause*) About what, Mrs Radford?

Sarah About what happened the night Jack was killed. I sometimes wonder whether I ... (*she changes her mind, almost as if she is frightened of her thoughts*) No! No! I mustn't say that ... I really mustn't! (*She moves away from him*) I'm sorry, I'm terribly sorry. I'm overwrought this morning. ... Forgive me ...

Cliff There's nothing to forgive. (*Pause*) I understand you're seeing a specialist on Monday—a Dr Trenchman.

Sarah Yes. Yes, I believe I am.

Cliff I've met Dr Trenchman. He's a very nice man.

Sarah (*nervously; shaking her head*) He may be but—I'm terrified of strange doctors. Always have been, ever since I was a little girl.

Cliff Yes, well—I can assure you, you won't be frightened of Dr Trench-man.

Sarah (*quietly*) We'll see. Now, if you'll excuse me, Superintendent. (*She moves down to the drinks cabinet*)

Pause

Cliff hesitates, then crosses to the hall. He is about to exit, then once again hesitates. He stands looking at her

Cliff It's just occurred to me. I shall be going up to London on Monday. If it's any help to you, I could very easily take you up to town and drive you back.

Sarah turns. Slight pause

Sarah That's very kind of you, but—

Cliff I'd like to do that. I really would. Anyway, think about it, and give me a ring. I'm in the book, Sarah.

Cliff exits

Sarah is taken aback by the use of her first name, and just a shade puzzled

The Lights fade to a Black-out

SCENE 4

The same. Six months later. Morning

Anna is sitting on the sofa drinking a cup of coffee. There are several books on the small table. After a little while she finishes the coffee, rises, and puts down the cup

Lucy enters

Lucy I'm very sorry, Miss Truman. I thought Mrs Radford would have been back ages ago.

Anna That's all right, Lucy. She wasn't expecting me, I just dropped in on the off chance. (*She glances at her watch*) But I'm afraid I can't wait any longer. (*She indicates the books*) I'm returning the books Mrs Radford lent me.

Lucy I'll see she gets them, Miss . . .

Anna And thank you for the coffee.

Lucy picks up the cup and collects the books

The door bell rings

Lucy That could be Mrs Radford now. She's a great one for forgetting her keys.

Lucy exits

Anna moves toward the hall

Pause

Arnold Boston enters with Lucy. He carries a brief-case

Arnold (*surprised*) Oh—good morning, Miss Truman!

Anna Hallo, Mr Boston. (*To Lucy*) Tell Mrs Radford I'll give her a ring some time this afternoon.

Lucy nods and exits

Arnold I haven't seen you recently, Miss Truman. Have you left Turnbulls?

Anna I'm on holiday at the moment.

Arnold Well, don't stay away too long, please! I have very little confidence in that other young lady.

Anna Maureen? (*She laughs*) She's really very capable.

Arnold She may be. But, oh dear—that purple hair-do and those ghastly clothes. She really should be working in a disco, not a pharmacy!

Anna She does work in a disco—five nights a week.

Arnold (*with a little laugh*) That explains a great deal . . .

Tiny pause

Anna How is Mrs Boston? Is she any better?

Arnold (*holding up crossed fingers*) I'm quite optimistic at the moment. (*Curiously*) I—I didn't realize you were a friend of Mrs Radford's?

Anna I was talked into joining the local Drama Club and Mrs Radford's the secretary . . .

Arnold Yes, of course . . .

Anna Both she and Mrs Warren have been very kind to me. Except that Katie Warren's now trying to talk me into playing Candida!

Arnold And why not? You'd make an excellent Candida.

Anna I doubt it. I doubt it very much! Well—if you'll excuse me, Mr Boston?

Arnold Yes, of course. Are you going away?

Anna I'm hoping to get away tomorrow.

Arnold Well—enjoy yourself.

Anna smiles at him and exits

Arnold moves down to one of the armchairs, makes himself comfortable, and opens his briefcase. He takes out a bulky document and proceeds to study it. Pause. He takes a pen out of his pocket and starts making corrections on the manuscript, puzzling over a clause in the document

Sarah rushes into the room. She is a shade breathless but looks considerably more relaxed than in the previous scenes

Arnold immediately puts his pen away, replaces the papers in his case, and rises

Sarah Arnold, I'm sorry! I'm terribly sorry!

Arnold That's all right, my dear.

Sarah I had to drive a friend of mine to the station and we got caught up in the most awful traffic jam.

Arnold Not to worry. I've only just arrived. But you've just missed Miss Truman . . .

Sarah Yes, I've seen her. I bumped into her.

Arnold (*a moment, then*) I must say, I was very surprised to find her here . . .

Sarah Were you, Arnold? Why?

Arnold Why?

Sarah Why were you surprised?

Arnold Well—in view of what you told me about Jack, I naturally assumed that you must have felt . . . (*he is faintly embarrassed, wishing he had never broached the subject*) Well, you know me, Sarah! I'm way behind the times on some things. Never will understand these modern relationships. Wouldn't touch a divorce case these days with a barge pole . . .

Sarah (*friendly*) There's nothing to understand. I met Anna and liked her. Most people do. Katie's very fond of her— they've become great buddies. I think you'd like her too, Arnold, if you really got to know her.

Arnold Probably, my dear. Very probably. (*He dismisses the subject*) I'm sorry I haven't contacted you lately, but I haven't been neglecting your affairs, I assure you. In fact, I do believe I've got some good news at long last. (*With a sudden thought*) That is of course, if you haven't changed your mind.

Sarah About Donnington's? No, I haven't changed my mind.

Arnold Good. I've been in touch with a firm called Blackstone and Harris ...

Sarah They're well known ...

Arnold Yes, and very sound financially, which is the important thing. They're definitely interested in a take-over, Sarah. Peter Blackstone's going to give you a ring and arrange a meeting.

Sarah Thank you, Arnold.

Arnold As soon as he's been in touch with you let me know and we'll take it from there. And if you do have second thoughts. ...

Sarah I shan't. I promise you. If Edward was alive I might think differently but ... I don't want the responsibility of Donnington's, not any longer.

Arnold (*patting her arm*) You're doing the right thing, my dear. I'm sure. (*He picks up his briefcase, hesitates, then:*) I had a drink with the Chief Constable the other day. He tells me the police still think there's a connection between Jack's murder and the Belton Green affair.

Sarah Is that what you think, Arnold?

Arnold I'm not sure what I think. Robbery may have been the motive. We know for a fact that Jack always carried a great deal of money around with him and his wallet was empty when the police found it. (*He shrugs*) Whether that's significant or not, I wouldn't know. (*Pause*) I gather you've been seeing quite a lot of Cliff Jordan since he left the force.

Sarah Yes, we've become quite good friends.

Arnold He's a clever man.

Sarah I think so.

Arnold He's going to make a name for himself, Sarah. A big name. I'm sure of that.

Sarah I hope you're right. He's certainly riding high at the moment. He's just finished a new book and he's off to New York very shortly.

Arnold Is he, by jove ...

Sarah *A Possible Explanation* has just been published in America and it's a great success. He's very thrilled.

Arnold I'm sure he is. What's the new book about, do you know?

Sarah (*amused*) Do I know? I've practically lived with it during the past couple of months. It's very much like the first one. A collection of unsolved murder cases.

Arnold Well, I wish him luck with it. You say he's off to the States?

Sarah Yes—at the end of the month.

Pause

Arnold Has he ... asked you to go with him?

Sarah Yes, he's asked me—in a roundabout way.

Arnold And what did you say, in a roundabout way?

Sarah I said no, Arnold.

Arnold Oh ...

Sarah You sound disappointed.

Arnold I like Cliff. Always have liked him. I should have second thoughts if I were you, Sarah.

Sarah Is that your professional advice?

Arnold Let's just say, it's the advice of an elderly romantic who has your best interests at heart.

Lucy enters

Lucy Excuse me, Madam. Mr Jordan's here . . .

Sarah (*a shade surprised*) Oh . . . Ask him to come in, Lucy. And Mrs Warren's borrowing my car. Give her the keys when she arrives. They're in the hall.

Lucy exits

Arnold Were you expecting Cliff?

Sarah Yes, but not for an hour or so. He's taking me out to lunch.

Arnold nods

Arnold Get in touch with me, Sarah, when you've heard from Peter Blackstone.

Cliff enters

Cliff Why, hallo, Arnold! Sarah, I'm sorry. I had no idea Arnold was with you. I hope I'm not interrupting . . .

Sarah That's all right, Cliff.

Arnold We've finished. I'm just off. (*He moves towards the hall*) We've just been talking about you, my friend, and this American trip of yours.

Cliff Oh—yes. (*Hesitantly*) I'm looking forward to it.

Sarah looks at him curiously

Arnold I'm sure you are. Give my love to New York. Irene and I spent our honeymoon there. We went over on the old *Queen Elizabeth*. Happy days . . .

Arnold exits

Sarah (*moving down to Cliff*) Has something happened?

Cliff Yes. I had a call from New York late last night. The publishers want me to go over straight away. They've arranged an interview with the *New York Times* and there's some talk of my going on television at the weekend. They're very excited about it.

Sarah I'm sure they are. Aren't you?

Cliff I—I don't know. I've got rather mixed feelings at the moment. It's all happening so quickly . . .

Sarah You're nervous?

Cliff Nervous? I'm terrified! At heart I'm still the local bobby.

Sarah Don't give me that routine! Save it for the Americans!

Cliff laughs

You're a cool, self-possessed charmer . . .

Cliff Only when I'm with you, Sarah . . .

Sarah When are you leaving?

Cliff Hopefully, the day after tomorrow. I'm on my way to the travel agents.

Sarah You must have a hundred and one things to see to. Why don't we forget our lunch?

Cliff No! That's the very last thing I want to do!

Sarah Are you sure?

Cliff I'm quite sure. Anyway, I didn't come here just to talk about the American trip . . .

Sarah No?

Cliff No. (*He takes a loose-leaf notebook out of his pocket*) I'd like you to read something, Sarah. Something I've written.

Sarah Yes, of course. What is it? Is it the short story you mentioned?

Cliff No, no, it's nothing like that . . .

As Cliff hesitates

Sarah Well—what is it?

Cliff (*a moment then:*) When I'd finished the new book I felt relieved and yet at the same time very much at a loose end.

Sarah nods

When you've worked hard on something it's almost an anti-climax when the job's finished. One morning I felt more restless than usual so I sat down at the typewriter and started making notes about . . . (*he hesitates*)

Sarah About what?

Cliff About your husband, about Anna Truman, Arnold Boston, Kate Warren, Dr Young—and all the things that happened here six months ago. I did my best to look at the sequence of events in a completely detached, analytical way—just as if I'd never met the people involved. As if I was devising another chapter of the book.

Sarah And did you succeed?

Slight pause

Cliff Yes, I think perhaps I did. Anyway, these are my notes.

Sarah What are you saying? That you have a theory? That you now know—or think you know—who killed Jack?

Cliff I'm simply asking you to read the notes I've made. That's all.

A moment—then Sarah takes the notebook from him

When you've read them I'll destroy the notebook. And I shall never mention it again. Never—I promise you.

Sarah (*staring at him, puzzled*) You promise me? I don't understand. (*Still staring at him, uneasily*) What is it, Cliff? (*Pause—then with almost a note of defiance in her voice*) What is it you're trying to say? That I killed Jack? Is that what you believe?

A strained silence

Cliff (*indicating the notebook she is holding*) I'd very much like you to read what I've written. Then you'll know what I believe—and what I think really happened the night your husband was killed.

Sarah's eyes are now on the book

I'll pick you up in about an hour.

Cliff exits

Sarah stands, a shade worried, looking towards the hall—then she moves down to the sofa. There is a peculiar intensity about her as she sits quietly reading Cliff's notes. There is a long pause while Sarah continues reading

Kate enters. She is holding Sarah's car keys

Kate Thanks for the car, Sarah. When shall I bring it back?

Sarah either doesn't hear her or takes no notice. Her eyes are still fixed on Cliff's notebook

Pause

When do you want the car back, Sarah?

Slight pause then Sarah looks up. She stares at Kate for a long moment, then:

Sarah I'm sorry, Kate. What did you say?
Kate (*puzzled*) I'm picking up the car. When do you want me to return it?
Sarah Oh—any time. It doesn't matter. Suit yourself.... (*She returns to the notebook*)
Kate (*moving down to Sarah*) Is tomorrow afternoon all right?
Sarah Yes ...
Kate They've promised to let me have my car back by lunch time, but you know what these garage people are like. They very rarely ... (*She realizes Sarah is not listening to her*) What is that, Sarah? What is it you're reading?
Sarah It's—it's nothing ...
Kate Don't be silly, darling. You're positively glued to it!
Sarah It's something Cliff asked me to read, that's all.
Kate (*surprised*) Cliff?
Sarah Yes.

Pause

Kate Well—what is it? You still haven't told me ...
Sarah It's—not important.
Kate Oh, come on! It must be, otherwise you wouldn't be so interested in it. (*A sudden thought strikes her*) Is it about Jack?
Sarah Why do you say that?
Kate I've just finished reading Cliff's book. *A Possible Explanation*, and I wondered if he'd come up with another "possible explanation" to do with Jack's murder?
Sarah No, no, it's nothing like that. (*She realizes she has to make an effort to stem Kate's curiosity*) Cliff's written a short story and he's asked me to read it.
Kate Oh. (*Not totally convinced*) Oh, I see.

Sarah rises and puts the notebook down on the arm of the chair

Sarah Where are you off to? I must say you look very elegant.
Kate I'm having lunch in town with some friends of mine.
Sarah Well, don't worry about the car. Keep it as long as you like.

The telephone rings. Sarah hesitates, then crosses to the table and picks up the phone

(*On the phone*) Hallo? ... Yes, this is Mrs Radford speaking. ... Oh, hallo, Mr Blackstone! ... Yes, Arnold said you'd be getting in touch with me. ... Of course, I'll be delighted to meet you. ... How long are you staying in London? ... I see. ... (*Pause*) That's very kind of you. ... Well, almost any day next week. ... Tuesday, one o'clock, at the Dorchester? ... That's fine. ... Yes, I'll certainly tell Arnold you telephoned. ... Thank you for ringing. ...

As Sarah replaces the receiver and turns away from the table she suddenly realizes that Kate has picked up the notebook and is looking at it

Kate! Give me that!
Kate (*astonished by her tone*) Sarah, please ...
Sarah Give me that notebook ...
Kate There's no need to shout at me!
Sarah Give it to me, Kate! (*She suddenly grabs hold of Kate's arm, attempting to take the notebook away from her*)

Kate is taken aback, but she holds on to the notebook

Kate Please let go of my arm!

A tense pause, then Sarah releases her arm and partly turns away from Kate

Sarah I'm sorry ... I'm terribly sorry, I just don't know what got into me! (*She turns towards her again*) Do forgive me, Katie ...

Kate stares at her for a moment, hesitates, then her curiosity gets the better of her and she opens the notebook. There is a long and uncomfortable silence, then:

Kate Are you the only one that's seen this?
Sarah Yes.
Kate Cliff hasn't shown it to anyone else?
Sarah No ...
Kate Are you sure?
Sarah I'm quite sure.

Kate slowly closes the notebook, then hands it to Sarah

Please don't worry, Katie. It's only what Cliff thinks. It's only his opinion. ... Just a theory. ... He's not going to discuss it with anyone, I assure you.
Kate Did he tell you that?
Sarah Yes. Yes, he did. ... He made a point of it.

Kate (*a moment, then:*) Very well, Sarah, We'll—talk about it tomorrow. I'll ring you in the morning.

Kate exits

Sarah is feeling the after-effects of her slight encounter with Kate. She puts the notebook down on the table and, crossing to the cabinet, pours herself a drink. She is about to pick up the drink when she suddenly finds herself looking up at the portrait of Jack Radford. She stares at the portrait for a long moment, then slowly raises the glass

Sarah Here's to Cliff! . . . Why? . . . Because he got it right, that's why! . . . (*Contemptuously*) Jack, my love!

The Lights fade until there is only a spotlight pin-pointing the notebook on the table. The spotlight stays on the notebook and after a tiny pause we hear Jack's (recorded) voice

Sarah moves to the sofa and lies down, asleep

Jack's Voice . . . Kate? It's Jack. . . . Katie, I wondered if you could drop in and see Sarah some time tomorrow? . . . She's frightfully depressed and unfortunately I'm spending tonight in London. . . . That's very sweet of you, I appreciate it . . . I should be back sometime in the afternoon. . . . No, no, don't ring her. I don't want her to think I've been in touch with you. . . . What's that, my dear? . . . It's difficult to say, I think perhaps she's worried about seeing the specialist, she's been talking about it most of the evening. . . . Thank you, Katie . . . Goodnight, my dear . . .

Jack enters

The spotlight fades and the Lights come up to reveal Jack by the table replacing the phone. He crosses into the sun-lounge, draws back the curtains, opens the patio door, and looks out into the garden. A pause—then he partly closes the door, and, obviously annoyed, returns to the sofa, and stands, looking down at Sarah

Jack exits into the hall. Pause

From another part of the house a clock can be heard chiming the hour. Nine o'clock

Sarah stirs, as if she has heard the clock striking, then moving her body into a more comfortable position goes back to sleep. Another pause

Jack enters. He now carries a nightdress

He puts the nightdress down, glances at Sarah, then returns to the sun-lounge. Once again he looks out into the garden. There is no sign of Anna

Jack (*to himself*) Anna, for God's sake, where are you? . . .

After a moment he crosses, picks up the nightdress, and moves cautiously towards the sofa . . . As he draws near to Sarah she suddenly comes to life, springing up from the sofa and facing him

(*Completely taken aback*) Sarah!

Sarah You were going to kill me!

Jack Kill you! What are you talking about?

Sarah There was something in the drink you gave me! Something to put me to sleep ...

Jack (*quickly; glibly*) Don't talk such nonsense!

Sarah (*moving away from him*) Ever since Edward died you've tried to make me commit suidice. .... You've done your best to convince people that I was going out of my mind. ...

Jack (*shaking his head*) You've been ill, Sarah. Very ill. ...

Sarah That's not true!

Jack It is true, Sarah, my love. ...

Sarah (*tensely*) You were going to put me to sleep, put the nightdress on me, and take me down to the pool. ... You wanted people to think that I'd gone there on the spur of the moment. ... That I'd finally killed myself ...

Jack Who told you that? Who told you such a ridiculous story? (*Suddenly realizing*) My God, you've been talking to Anna!

Sarah Yes, I've been talking to Anna! Not only that—I showed her a letter I found. A letter from Carol Hoskins. It was in your blazer. As soon as she realized there was someone else—that you'd simply been making use of her—she told me about the pills and what actually happened that night you brought her here. ...

Jack (*stopping her; intensely angry*) The bitch! The stupid little bitch!

Sarah At first I didn't believe her. I just couldn't believe that you'd do such a terrible thing! But I was determined to find out!

Jack Well—you've found out! (*He snatches up the glass which is on the table*) Now do as I tell you! Drink this!

Sarah shakes her head and backs further away from him

You heard what I said! (*He offers her the glass*) Drink it. ...

Sarah gives a terrified shake of the head and retreats further, into the sun-lounge

Jack picks up the knife from the table and quickly moves forward, threatening her with it

Do as I say! Drink it!

Sarah No, I'm not going to!

Jack Drink it!

Sarah hesitates, her eyes on the knife, paralysed with terror—then with a sharp intake of breath she takes the glass out of his hand

Pause

Jack watches her as she raises the glass to her lips. She is just about to drink ...

Anna suddenly enters from the patio

Jack turns, thunderstruck by Anna's appearance. As he turns Sarah springs forward and tosses the contents of the glass into his face. With a cry of anger he drops the knife, lashes out at Sarah, and as she stumbles to the floor covers his face with his hands. Anna has quickly taken in the scene and she rushes towards Jack in a desperate attempt to stop him from retrieving the knife. There is a tense struggle. Anna has almost got possession of the knife when Jack changes his tactics and, releasing her arm, reaches for her throat. He is attempting to throttle her when Anna, in anger and self-defence, plunges the knife into his body. Jack releases his grip, staggers, then collapses. Sarah has slowly recovered and joins Anna. They stand staring down at Jack's body, horrified by the turn of events.

Anna (*with barely controlled hysteria*) . . . Is he dead? . . . Have I killed him?

Pause

Sarah makes a determined effort to take command of the situation. She kneels down by Jack and briefly examines him

Pause

Sarah rises, hesitates, then gives Anna a little nod

    I wish to God I hadn't come here! I wish I hadn't come . . . ! (*In tears*) But I promised you I would . . . and I was so angry with him. . . . So angry. . . .

Sarah Thank God, you did come! If you hadn't, he'd have killed me. . . .

Anna But—what are we going to do? (*She is panic stricken*) Are you going to send for the police?

A strained silence

Sarah (*thoughtfully*) No, Anna—I'm not going to send for the police. . . .

Anna Then—what's going to happen?

Sarah stares at Anna for a long moment, then she makes a decision

Sarah Now listen! And listen carefully! (*She moves nearer to Anna and takes hold of her arm*) I'll take responsibility for what's happened! You never came here! You understand? (*Pause*) You understand Anna?

Anna (*softly*) Yes. . . .

Sarah (*releasing her*) Now you must help me take him into the garden . . .

Anna (*facing her; bewildered*) The garden? Why? Why the garden?

Sarah We must make it look as if Jack saw someone—a stranger—and went to investigate.

Anna But supposing someone. . . .

Sarah (*stopping her*) Anna, please! You've got to trust me! You've got to do exactly what I tell you! (*She crosses towards the hall*)

Anna (*alarmed*) Where are you going?

Sarah We need a blanket. Just wait here—and don't touch anything! (*Tensely*) Don't touch anything!

    Sarah exits

Pause

As Anna stands terrified, staring down at the body . . . The Lights slowly fade to a Black-out

In the Black-out Anna and Jack exit and Sarah and Cliff enter

The Lights gradually come up to reveal Sarah sitting on the sofa, staring at the open notebook which is now on her lap. Cliff has entered from the patio and, unknown to Sarah, is watching her. Pause. Sarah gradually becomes aware of his presence

Cliff You've read my notes?

Pause

Sarah Yes. Yes, I've read them.
Cliff Well Sarah?

The awkward silence continues, then:

There's nothing for you to worry about. Absolutely nothing. (*With almost an undertone of apology*) It's only a theory of mine remember—and I could be wrong.
Sarah (*quietly, as she rises*) Yes, but—you're not wrong, Cliff. It's what happened. (*She looks at the notebook again*) It's exactly what happened that night . . .
Cliff (*moving down to her*) I'm sorry if I've upset you. That wasn't my intention. But I thought it only fair to you—and to myself—that you should know what I've been thinking, what's been at the back of my mind. Your husband was determined to kill you. I'm convinced of that, and no one will ever convince me otherwise—but I'm also convinced that *after* he was murdered you deliberately gave me, and everyone else, the impression that you were still on the verge of a breakdown. A woman constantly imagining things, and utterly incapable of telling the truth about anything. (*A moment*) And that just wasn't true. That wasn't the case. Was it Sarah?
Sarah No, it wasn't . . .
Cliff You wanted to divert attention from Anna. You knew that if I once suspected her, and got tough, she'd probably lose her nerve. . . .
Sarah (*nodding*) When I told Anna I intended to put her story to the test and find out, once and for all, whether my husband really did intend to kill me—she offered to help. She said she'd even join forces with me and confront Jack, if necessary. At the time I didn't think she meant it, but I was wrong.
Cliff I had a hunch, right at the beginning, that you were shielding someone. I thought at first that Kate Warren was involved and then, about a week or so ago, I bumped into Anna Truman. I reminded her of our previous meeting, when I was with the force—and she immediately took fright. From that moment onwards I became curious and started making inquiries about her. Amongst other things I discovered that she'd left Turnbulls and had booked a flight to Australia.
Sarah (*softly*) She's thinking of emigrating.

Cliff Yes, I know . . .

Pause

Sarah (*lamely*) She has a married sister in Melbourne . . .

Cliff nods. Sarah looks at him, hesitantly. Pause

What's going to happen, Cliff? What are you going to do?
Cliff Do? About what?
Sarah This—theory of yours?
Cliff But you know what I'm going to do! I've already told you. (*He takes the notebook from her*)

They face each other for a brief moment, then he tears the notebook into pieces, crosses to the desk, and drops it into the wastepaper basket. When he returns to Sarah his manner has changed slightly, there is now a suggestion of both urgency and authority

Time is short, and I'm sure you've a great many things to attend to before we leave for the States on Wednesday morning. So I suggest this afternoon we both . . .
Sarah We?
Cliff Yes! We . . .
Sarah No, Cliff! I told you I can't possibly . . .
Cliff (*stopping her*) You're coming with me, Sarah! You've got to come! For my sake—if for no other reason. I just won't take no for an answer!

Sarah shakes her head

Sarah, look at me! (*He displays a distinctly unsteady hand*) Your cool self-possessed charmer is scared to death, he's shaking like a leaf! What on earth do you think is going to happen to me in New York if I feel like this now? You've just got to come! I need you. (*A moment; then he gently touches her*) I shall always need you.

Pause

Sarah I—I don't know whether I . . . can be ready in time . . .
Cliff You'll be ready! You'll be ready and you'll never regret it. Never! I promise you—Sarah, my love . . .

A strange look flickers across Sarah's face as Cliff gently takes her in his arms

Black-out

CURTAIN

FURNITURE AND PROPERTY LIST

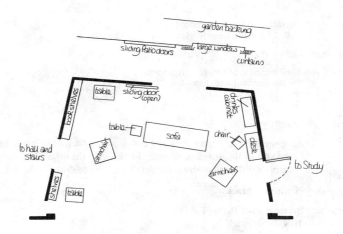

ACT 1

SCENE 1

On stage: Desk with drawers
Table. *On it:* telephone, private telephone book, ashtray, cigarette box
Coffee tables. *On them:* table lamps
Drinks cabinet. *On it:* An assortment of bottles and glasses, including a
    decanter of sherry and brandy
Large portrait of Jack Radford
Works of art
Leather-bound volumes of the classics
Sofa
Armchairs
Wastepaper basket
Rug and cushions in the sun-lounge
Curtains

Off stage: Several sheets of notepaper **(Lucy)**
Outdoor clothes **(Lucy)**
Folder of letters **(Jack)**

Personal: **Geoffrey:** pair of glasses, briefcase
Jack: coat, gun loaded with blanks

SCENE 2

Strike: Dirty glasses

Personal: **Kate:** Headscarf
    Jack: raincoat, tiny bottle of tablets in jacket pocket
    Anna: neck chain
    Maurice: wristwatch, doctor's bag

SCENE 3

Strike: Cigarette stub, wet raincoat
    N.B. Leave the brandy glass on the drinks cabinet

Off stage;   Duster **(Lucy)**

Personal: **Maurice:** doctor's bag, wristwatch
    Sarah: pendant necklace

SCENE 4

Strike: Brandy glass

Set: An assortment of letters, bills and envelopes and a stiletto paper-knife on the arm of the armchair, a drink for Jack on the other arm and a near empty drink for Sarah on the small table by the side of the sofa

Off stage: Nightdress **(Jack)**

Personal: **Sarah:** sewing (hem of skirt)
    Jack: wristwatch

SCENE 5

Strike: Dirty glasses, Sarah's sewing, nightdress

Personal: **Lucy:** handkerchief

ACT II
SCENE 1

Off stage: Cup of tea **(Lucy)**

Personal: **Cliff:** jotter in pocket
    Arnold: document case
    Sarah: pendant necklace

SCENE 2

Off stage: Tray with legs. *On it:* elaborate meal including melba toast and a slim vase holding a single rose **(Kate)**

Personal: **Sarah:** dressing-gown
    Geoffrey: pair of glasses, handkerchief

SCENE 3

Strike: Tray

Cup of coffee by armchair

Personal: **Maurice:** doctor's bag, morning newspaper, wristwatch
Sarah: small bottle of capsules

SCENE 4

Strike: Dirty coffee cup

Set: Cup of coffee by sofa, several books on the small table, glass on table,
correspondence and knife on small table

Off stage: Nightdress **(Jack)**

Personal: **Anna:** wristwatch
Arnold: briefcase containing a bulky document, pen in pocket
Cliff: loose-leaf notebook in pocket
Kate: Sarah's car keys

LIGHTING PLOT

Property fittings required: several lamps, light switch in sun-lounge

Interior.   A living room and sun-lounge. The same scene throughout

ACT I, SCENE 1.   Late afternoon
To open: General interior lighting

Cue 1	**Edward** slumps forward on the sofa	(Page 10)
	Black-out	

ACT I, SCENE 2.   Evening

To open: General interior lighting

Cue 2	**Jack** switches off the lights	(Page 21)
	Black-out the sun-lounge	
Cue 3	**Jack:** "Nine o'clock, Anna! No later!"	(Page 21)
	Lights fade to black-out	

ACT I, SCENE 3.   Morning

To open: General interior lighting

Cue 4	**Sarah:** "Its just that I want to change my will ..."	(Page 28)
	Lights fade to black-out	

ACT I, SCENE 4.   Evening

To open: General interior lighting

Cue 5	As **Jack** moves cautiously towards **Sarah**	(Page 31)
	Lights slowly fade to black-out	

ACT I, SCENE 5.   Morning

To open: General interior lighting

Cue 6	**Geoffrey** stares at **Cliff**, incredulously	(Page 35)
	Lights fade	

ACT II, SCENE 1.   Morning

To open: General interior lighting

Cue 7	**Sarah** is staring at **Cliff**	(Page 46)
	Lights fade to black-out	

ACT II, Scene 2.   Evening

To open: General interior lighting

Cue 8   **Sarah** stares back . . . cold and unfriendly   (Page 52)
         Lights slowly fade to black-out

ACT II Scene 3.   Morning

To open: General interior lighting

Cue 9   **Sarah** is just a shade puzzled   (Page 58)
         Lights fade to black-out

ACT II Scene 4.   Morning

To open: General interior lighting

Cue 10   **Sarah:** "Jack, my love!"   (Page 66)
         Lights fade to spotlight pinpointing the notebook on the table

Cue 11   **Jack** enters   (Page 66)
         Spotlight fades. Lights up to evening level

Cue 12   As **Anna** stands terrified   (Page 69)
         Lights slowly fade to black-out

Cue 13   **Sarah** enters   (Page 69)
         Lights gradually come up

Cue 14   **Cliff** gently takes her in his arms   (Page 70)
         Black-out

EFFECTS PLOT

Practicals required: opening/closing front door

ACT I

Cue 1   **Sarah:** "I don't know how she manages it."   (Page 2)
         Telephone rings

Cue 2   As **Jack** reaches the table   (Page 8)
         Piano playing in the studio

Cue 3   **Jack** dials a long-distance number. Pause   (Page 8)
         Piano music ceases

Cue 4   As Scene 2 opens   (Page 11)
         Sound of rain, continuing

Cue 5   As **Sarah** draws her dressing-gown closer to her body (Page 11)
         Front door bell

Cue 6   **Jack** releases **Anna**   (Page 18)
         Front door bell

Cue 7   **Jack** returns the cushions to the sun-lounge   (Page 18)
         Front door bell

Cue 8   **Jack** exits into the hall. Pause   (Page 30)
         Clock chimes, nine o'clock

ACT II

Cue 9   **Sarah** starts to laugh   (Page 40)
         Front door bell

Cue 10   **Sarah** turns and looks towards the sound. Pause   (Page 50)
         Front door bell

Cue 11   **Lucy** collects the books   (Page 58)
         Front door bell

Cue 12   **Sarah:** "Keep it as long as you like."   (Page 65)
         Telephone rings

Cue 13   Lights fade until . . . table. Tiny pause   (Page 66)
         Jack's recorded voice (as script p. 66)

Cue 14   **Jack** exits into the hall. Pause   (Page 66)
         Clock chimes nine o'clock

MADE AND PRINTED IN GREAT BRITAIN BY
LATIMER TREND & COMPANY LTD PLYMOUTH

MADE IN ENGLAND